Autonomous Security

Valarian Couch

Published by Valarian Couch, 2023.

AUTONOMOUS SECURITY

First edition. December 30, 2023.

ISBN: 979-8223972884

Written by Valarian Couch.

AUTONOMOUS SECURITY

THE RISE OF AI IN SELF-DEFENDING NETWORKS

AUTHOR'S NAME: VALARIAN COUCH

Foreword

Welcome to ***"AUTONOMOUS SECURITY: THE RISE OF AI IN SELF-DEFENDING NETWORKS."*** This book is an exciting journey into the world of cybersecurity and artificial intelligence (AI), two fields that are rapidly changing how we protect our digital lives.

In the digital age, security is more important than ever. Every day, we hear about new cyber-attacks and threats. These threats aren't just against big companies; they can affect anyone, from individuals to small businesses. That's why understanding how to defend against these threats is so important.

This is where AI comes in. AI isn't just for science fiction movies; it's real, and it's here to help us. In this book, we'll explore how AI is being used to create networks that can defend themselves. These networks are smart. They can learn, adapt, and respond to threats much faster than humans can. It's like having a super-smart guard dog for your computer network, always watching and ready to act.

We'll start by understanding the basics: what is AI, and why is it so important in cybersecurity? Don't worry, we won't get lost in complicated terms. The goal is to make this as clear and simple as possible

Next, we'll dive into the history of network security. How did we get here? What were the steps that led to the development of AI in security? This part is like a time machine, showing us how past events shape our present and future

Then, we'll look at the current state of self-defending networks. What are they, how do they work, and why are they so effective? We'll also discuss the challenges and limitations because, like anything else, AI isn't perfect.

Finally, we'll dream about the future. What's next for AI and cybersecurity? How will these technologies continue to evolve and protect us? Whether you're a student, a professional, or just someone curious about AI and cybersecurity, this book is for you. We hope to provide you with valuable insights, answer your questions, and spark your interest in these fascinating fields.

So, let's begin this journey together. Turn the page, and let's dive into Autonomous security and AI.

Acknowledgments

Writing this book has been an incredible journey, and it wouldn't have been possible without the support and encouragement of many people.

First and foremost, I want to express my deepest gratitude to my family. Your unwavering belief in my vision and constant support provided the foundation upon which this book was built. To my wife, for your patience and love, and to my children, who remind me every day of the importance of pursuing one's passions – thank you from the bottom of my heart.

A special thanks goes to my colleagues and peers in the cybersecurity and AI communities. Your insights, feedback, and spirited discussions have been invaluable. I am particularly grateful to my mentor in late memory of Anthony Brown, whose mentorship and wisdom have been guiding lights in my career. Your perspective on the evolving world of cybersecurity has been a major inspiration for this book.

Lastly, to you, the readers, who share a keen interest in the world of AI and cybersecurity – this book is for you. Your eagerness to learn and evolve in this ever-changing field is what drives authors like myself to share our knowledge and experiences. I hope this book provides you with valuable insights and aids in your journey in cybersecurity.

Thank you all for being part of this incredible journey.

VALARIAN COUCH

INTRODUCTION TO CYBERSECURITY

In today's digital era, cybersecurity faces an ever-growing wave of sophisticated threats. This challenge has paved the way for Artificial Intelligence (AI) to become a cornerstone in cybersecurity strategies. AI in cybersecurity is about equipping digital systems with intelligent, self-learning technology that goes beyond traditional defense mechanisms.

AI in cybersecurity functions as a dynamic protector, continuously learning from vast amounts of data that include both typical network activities and cyber threats. This process, known as machine learning, enables AI systems to distinguish between normal and malicious activities effectively. Unlike conventional security methods reliant on static rules, AI's strength lies in its ability to adapt and evolve, making it particularly effective against new and emerging threats.

One of AI's most crucial capabilities in cybersecurity is pattern recognition. It meticulously analyzes data to identify anomalies that could signal potential breaches, such as unusual login attempts or unexpected patterns in the data flow. This capability isn't just reactive but also predictive. AI analyzes trends to foresee and preempt potential security threats, allowing organizations to take proactive measures.

The real-time response is another area where AI shines in cybersecurity. Upon detecting a threat, AI systems can immediately take steps to mitigate it, often neutralizing dangers before they can inflict significant damage. This instantaneous response is vital in a landscape where even a few minutes delay can lead to substantial losses.

Furthermore, AI's adaptability in cybersecurity is unparalleled. Cyber threats are continually evolving, but AI keeps pace by constantly updating its understanding of threat patterns. This adaptability extends across various cybersecurity areas, including threat detection, incident response, risk management, and user behavior analytics. AI doesn't just recognize known viruses and malware; it's also proficient in identifying and responding to sophisticated, previously unseen cyber-attacks.

In essence, AI's role in cybersecurity marks a transformative shift from the traditional, rule-based defense systems to a more intelligent, anticipatory, and responsive approach. By integrating AI into cybersecurity measures, we are not just employing a tool; we are adopting a fundamental change in how we protect our digital realms against the increasingly complex landscape of cyber threats.

Historical context and evolution of network security

Network security hasn't always been as complex and advanced as it is today. Its evolution is a tale of constant adaptation to the ever-changing landscape of technology and cyber threats.

Enhancing network security has become a crucial concern for all businesses and organizations in the present day. Tracing the origins of network security back to around 1950, it emerged concurrently with the recognition of the inherent worth of data. This realization evolved through various milestones as the Information and Digital Age progressed throughout the latter half of the 20th century.

During the late 1960s and early 1970s, the concept of digital storage emerged. This data was stored on massive mainframes that occupied entire rooms. To access the stored information, one had to physically connect to the mainframe or use terminals located within the same building. Initially, safeguarding confidential company data was not a significant concern, as physical presence in the building was required to access the information. The 1980s brought a revolution – the birth of the modern Internet. As more computers got connected, the network's boundaries expanded, and so did the security risks. The first notable incident was the Morris Worm in 1988, a program that unintentionally caused widespread damage to the early Internet. This incident was a wake-up call, highlighting the need for better security measures.

In response to growing threats, the 1990s saw the rise of the first firewalls and antivirus software. Firewalls acted like gatekeepers, controlling incoming and outgoing network traffic based on predetermined security rules. Antivirus software began to scan computers for known malicious programs and protect against them.

Less than a decade later, a pivotal shift occurred in how we viewed data as we entered the new millennium. Both network security threats and security measures became more sophisticated. The Internet is now a part of everyday life, and cyber-attacks have become more frequent and complex. This era saw the emergence of different security solutions, like intrusion detection systems (IDS) and intrusion prevention systems (IPS), designed to actively identify and block potential threats. As vast amounts of data were being stored digitally, it became clear that this data was not just a collection of numbers and facts. It had immense value, encompassing a wide range of personally identifiable information — from credit card data and bank account numbers to profit and loss statements, personal details, and demographic information on large population groups. Information began to be seen as a commodity, a valuable asset that needed stringent protection.

These developments marked the early beginnings of the future of network security, driven by the data revolution. It's a trend that continues to shape our approach to security. Consider this: it's projected that just five years from now, our collective global data will reach a staggering 175 zettabytes. To grasp the enormity of a zettabyte, picture the number 175 followed by 21 zeros. This immense volume of digital data will encompass everything from databases to videos, photos, apps, and much more.

As the amount of digital data proliferated rapidly, so did the risk of sensitive information fall into the wrong hands. This era of unprecedented data growth brought new challenges to network security, demanding innovative solutions and strategies to protect this valuable asset.

By the 2010s, cybersecurity had become a discipline in its own right. The focus shifted from just defending the perimeter (like with firewalls) to securing data wherever it resided. This was the era of big data breaches, which showed that the stakes were higher than ever. Cybersecurity now means protecting not just networks but also the data and identities of individuals and organizations.

Today, as the complexity and volume of cyber threats have exploded, traditional security measures alone are no longer enough. AI is the new frontier in network security. With its ability to learn from data, identify patterns, and make decisions, AI offers a dynamic and proactive approach to security. It's not just about defending against known threats anymore; it's about predicting and preventing future threats.

CHAPTER 1: UNDERSTANDING AUTONOMOUS SECURITY

1.1. What is an Autonomous System?

Autonomous Security refers to the self-governing capabilities of security systems enabled by Artificial Intelligence (AI) and Machine Learning (ML). These systems can independently detect, analyze, and respond to potential security threats without human intervention. This concept is a paradigm shift from traditional security measures that rely heavily on manual oversight and rule-based operations.

Autonomous security is a revolutionary concept in the field of cybersecurity, characterized by the use of advanced technologies, particularly artificial intelligence (AI), to enable security systems to operate independently with minimal human intervention. This innovation marks a radical departure from traditional security frameworks, which heavily relied on human oversight and manual processes. In autonomous security, the systems are not only self-sufficient in identifying and responding to threats but are also capable of learning and evolving over time.

At the heart of autonomous security is the idea of self-regulation and proactive defense mechanisms. Unlike conventional systems that work based on predefined rules and human-set parameters, autonomous security systems employ sophisticated algorithms that analyze data, learn from it, and make decisions based on this continuous learning process. These systems are designed to recognize patterns, detect anomalies, and respond to threats in real time, significantly reducing the window of opportunity for cyber attackers.

The transformative power of autonomous security lies in its ability to adapt to the ever-changing landscape of cyber threats. Traditional security measures often lag behind in the rapidly evolving digital world, where new threats emerge more quickly than they can be manually analyzed and addressed. Autonomous security systems, however, are built to adapt. They integrate machine learning, data analytics, and advanced pattern recognition to understand and anticipate new types of cyberattacks, making them far more effective than static, rule-based systems.

Furthermore, autonomous security addresses one of the most critical challenges in cybersecurity: the volume and complexity of data. In today's digital environment, the sheer amount of data generated and the complexity of networks can be overwhelming for traditional security systems and security professionals. Autonomous systems, with their capacity to process and analyze large datasets rapidly, offer a scalable and efficient solution. They can sift through vast amounts of information, identify relevant patterns, and isolate potential threats with a level of precision and speed that is unattainable for human operators.

Another significant aspect of autonomous security is its proactive stance. Traditional security systems are often reactive, springing into action only after a security breach has occurred. In contrast, autonomous security systems are designed to predict and prevent attacks before they happen. By constantly analyzing network traffic and user behavior, these systems can identify potential vulnerabilities and threats before they are exploited.

In essence, autonomous security represents a new era in cybersecurity, one where systems are not just reactive tools but intelligent, proactive guardians of digital integrity. This approach not only enhances the effectiveness of security measures but also reshapes the role of cybersecurity professionals, allowing them to focus on more strategic tasks while autonomous systems handle routine monitoring and response. As cyber threats become more sophisticated, the role of autonomous security becomes increasingly vital, representing the forefront of innovation in protecting digital assets and information in an increasingly interconnected world.

1.2. The Role of AI in Shaping Autonomous Security Solutions

The integration of Artificial Intelligence (AI) in the realm of autonomous security solutions marks a revolutionary leap in how we approach and manage cybersecurity. AI's influence in this area is profound, reshaping the very foundations of network security and offering unprecedented capabilities in the protection of digital infrastructures.

At its core, AI's role in autonomous security is about enhancing the intelligence and responsiveness of security systems. These systems, powered by AI, are not just reactive mechanisms but proactive entities capable of predicting, identifying, and neutralizing cyber threats with minimal human intervention. This transformation is achieved through several key functions of AI:

1. **Advanced Threat Detection:** AI algorithms are adept at analyzing patterns within vast quantities of data, a task impractical for humans to perform with the same efficiency. In autonomous security solutions, AI continuously scans network traffic, system logs, and user behaviors, searching for anomalies that might indicate a security threat. Unlike traditional security measures that rely on known threat signatures, AI-driven systems can detect novel or evolving threats, including zero-day exploits, by recognizing patterns

and anomalies that deviate from established norms.

2. **Predictive Analytics and Threat Intelligence:** AI extends beyond mere detection; it predicts future threats by analyzing trends and patterns. By processing and learning from historical data, including past attacks and breaches, AI can forecast potential security vulnerabilities and pre-emptively suggest protective measures. This predictive capability is crucial for staying ahead of cyber attackers who continuously evolve their methods.
3. **Automated Incident Response:** Upon detecting a threat, AI-driven autonomous security systems can instantly respond. This response can range from isolating affected systems to deploying patches or updating firewalls. The speed of this automated response is critical, often making the difference between a minor security incident and a major breach. AI's capability to analyze the severity and nature of the threat ensures that the response is not just swift but also appropriate to the specific challenge.
4. **Self-Learning and Adaptation:** One of the most significant aspects of AI in autonomous security is its ability to learn and adapt. By employing machine learning algorithms, these systems refine their detection and response mechanisms over time, learning from new data, threats, and interactions. This continuous learning process ensures that the security system evolves, becoming more adept at handling new and complex threats, thus maintaining robust security over time.
5. **Reducing False Positives:** A perennial challenge in cybersecurity is the high rate of false positives – benign activities mistakenly flagged as threats, leading to unnecessary or counterproductive responses. AI significantly reduces false positives by learning the normal operational patterns of a network and being able to distinguish between legitimate

anomalies and routine deviations.

6. **Customization and Scalability:** AI-driven security systems offer a high degree of customization, tailoring their operations to the specific needs and architecture of the network they protect. This customization is dynamic, with AI constantly adjusting its parameters based on ongoing network activity and changes. Furthermore, AI systems are inherently scalable and capable of expanding their protective coverage in tandem with the growth of the network infrastructure.
7. **Human-AI Collaboration:** While AI plays a pivotal role in autonomous security, it does not entirely replace human oversight. Instead, it augments human capabilities, handling routine and repetitive tasks while escalating complex issues for human analysis. This collaborative approach maximizes the strengths of both AI and human intelligence, ensuring a more robust and nuanced security posture.

CHAPTER 2: EVOLUTION OF NETWORK SECURITY

The evolution of network security is a fascinating journey that mirrors the development and expansion of computer networks and the Internet. In the earliest days of computing, before the 1970s, security concerns were largely confined to physical infrastructure and internal threats, as computers were either standalone units or operated in closed networks. These early systems, used primarily in academic, corporate, and military settings, prioritized information integrity and reliability over external security threats, largely because the concept of a widespread network was still in its infancy.

The landscape began to shift with the development of ARPANET in the late 1960s, a project of the United States Department of Defense. ARPANET laid the groundwork for today's internet, connecting multiple computers and allowing them to communicate. Initially, the network was limited to a few institutions, and users were a small, trusted group. Security was not a major concern; the focus was on making the network operational and reliable. However, as the network expanded and the number of users grew, the potential for misuse and external threats became apparent.

One of the first major wake-up calls came in 1988 with the Morris Worm. This was one of the first computer worms distributed via a network, causing significant disruption and bringing to light the vulnerabilities inherent in connected systems. This incident underscored the need for network security and marked the beginning of a more concerted effort to protect computer systems and networks from external threats.

As we entered the 1990s, the proliferation of personal computers and the advent of the World Wide Web opened up a new era in network security. This period saw the rise of viruses and malware, prompting the development and widespread adoption of antivirus software. Alongside this, the concept of firewalls evolved, moving from basic packet filters to more sophisticated systems capable of stateful inspection and, later, application-layer filtering. These were necessary advancements as the internet began to play a more significant role in both business and personal life, leading to a broader range of cyber threats.

The 2000s were marked by an explosion in internet use and the diversification of threats. Cybersecurity had to evolve rapidly to keep pace with challenges like spyware, adware, phishing, and more sophisticated forms of malware. The emergence of Advanced Persistent Threats (APTs) required a shift in focus from not just defending perimeters but also detecting and mitigating threats that had bypassed initial defenses. This era saw the rise of intrusion detection and prevention systems (IDS/IPS) that monitored network traffic to identify suspicious activities.

However, it was in the 2010s that a significant paradigm shift occurred with the introduction of artificial intelligence (AI) in network security. The explosion of big data and increasingly complex network architectures exposed the limitations of traditional security methods. Machine learning and AI began to be integrated into security systems, offering the ability to analyze vast datasets to detect patterns and anomalies. This capability marked the beginning of a new era in network security, one where systems could learn from past incidents, adapt to new threats, and predict vulnerabilities.

AI-powered security solutions revolutionized network security. Automated threat detection using AI algorithms could analyze data at a scale and speed impossible for human operators, leading to more efficient and effective threat detection. Predictive analytics further enhanced security measures, allowing organizations to anticipate and mitigate potential vulnerabilities before they were exploited.

Today, AI is a central component of network security. Modern networks are more autonomous and capable of self-diagnosis and self-healing in the face of security threats. This shift towards AI-driven, self-defending networks represents a significant leap in our ability to protect digital assets and maintain the integrity of our systems.

Looking ahead, the future of network security is poised for further transformation. Emerging technologies like quantum computing and the evolving nature of cyber threats will continue to shape network security strategies. The focus is likely to shift towards more proactive and predictive security measures, potentially leading to fully autonomous security management systems. This evolution, mirroring the growth and sophistication of networks and the threats they face, underscores the ever-changing and dynamic nature of network security.

CHAPTER 3: FUNDAMENTALS OF AI IN SECURITY

3.1. Overview

Artificial Intelligence (AI) combines various scientific disciplines, and developments in machine learning and deep learning significantly shape its growth. These advancements are revolutionizing almost every aspect of the technology industry, marking a major shift in how we approach and use technology across different sectors. At its essence, AI is about mimicking human cognitive functions. It's about creating systems that can perform tasks that would ordinarily require human intelligence. These tasks include speech recognition, decision-making, visual perception, and language translation.

History of Artificial Intelligence

Although the term "artificial intelligence" is not new, it has become a buzzword in recent years. In 1956, a group of avant-garde experts from various backgrounds decided to organize a summer AI research project. John McCarthy (Dartmouth College), Marvin Minsky (Harvard University), Nathaniel Rochester (IBM), and Claude Shannon (Bell Telephone Laboratories) led the project. This event marked the recognition of AI as an academic discipline.

3.2. Why is AI Important in Keeping Computers Safe?

Here's the thing: hackers and cybercriminals are always coming up with new tricks. It's hard for humans to keep up with them all the time. That's where AI comes in. It can learn and remember way more than any human can. So, it helps find and stop these sneaky cyber threats faster than we ever could.

Think of AI as your ultra-smart digital sidekick. It never gets tired or needs a break. Day and night, it's on the job, scanning the digital world for anything unusual. It's like a vigilant guard, always on the lookout for anything that doesn't seem right. And the best part? It learns from its experiences. If AI ever misses a cyber threat, it studies that mistake, learns how to spot it next time, and becomes even better at its job. It's always evolving and getting smarter, which is super important in the ever-changing landscape of cyber threats.

For those working in cybersecurity, AI is like a superhero's trusted ally. It does a lot of the legwork, sifting through mountains of data to pinpoint potential dangers. This helps cybersecurity professionals concentrate on the really challenging problems that need a human's intuition and decision-making skills.

In simple terms, AI in cybersecurity is our digital defender, always adapting and learning to keep our online world safe. It's like having a super-intelligent friend who's always got your back in the world of the internet. With AI on our side, we can feel a bit more secure knowing that our digital universe is being watched over by such advanced and ever-improving technology.

3.3. Core Concepts of AI in Security

- **Data Analysis:**

The foundation of AI's effectiveness in cybersecurity lies in its ability to handle vast and complex datasets. Cybersecurity AI systems depend on a myriad of data types, ranging from network traffic logs and user activity to historical records of security breaches and threat patterns. This data is crucial as it trains the AI to recognize and understand the landscape of cybersecurity threats. The AI algorithms excel at sifting through this data, extracting critical patterns and anomalies that might signal potential risks. Unlike traditional methods, which might take considerable time to analyze data, AI systems can process and interpret these vast datasets in real-time. This swift analysis is vital in detecting active security threats, allowing for instantaneous responses and mitigations.

- **Pattern Recognition and Anomaly Detection**

A core strength of AI in cybersecurity is its inherent capability to detect patterns and anomalies that deviate from the norm. This capability is not static; through machine learning, AI systems continuously evolve, enhancing their proficiency in identifying complex and subtle behavioral patterns. This evolution is particularly crucial in adapting to new and emerging cyber threats that traditional, signature-based detection methods might miss. Signature-based systems, which rely on known threat databases, often fall short of novel or sophisticated cyber threats. AI, however, through its advanced pattern recognition, can identify these threats by analyzing deviations from established patterns, thereby offering a more robust defense against a wider array of cyber-attacks.

- **Predictive Analytics and Proactive Security**

Another pivotal concept introduced by AI in cybersecurity is predictive analytics. AI systems can analyze historical data and current trends to predict potential future threats and vulnerabilities. This aspect of AI enables a more proactive approach to cybersecurity, moving beyond reactive measures. Predictive analytics in AI doesn't just fortify defenses against known threats; it prepares and adapts to potential future risks, allowing cybersecurity professionals to stay a step ahead of cybercriminals.

- **Machine Learning:**

The adaptability of AI in cybersecurity is largely attributed to machine learning. This dynamic aspect of AI involves models that learn and improve from experience without being explicitly programmed for every specific task. In the context of cybersecurity, this means that AI systems can learn from new data, adapt to changing threat landscapes, and enhance their decision-making processes over time. This continuous learning and adaptation make AI an indispensable ally in the ever-evolving field of cybersecurity, ensuring that defensive measures evolve in tandem with the advancing tactics of cyber adversaries.

- **Enhanced Threat Intelligence and Automated Decision-Making**

AI's capability extends to developing enhanced threat intelligence. By aggregating and analyzing data from various sources, AI systems offer a comprehensive view of the threat landscape. This intelligence is not just broad but also deep, providing insights into the nature, tactics, and potential impact of various threats. AI's role in cybersecurity is not limited to detection; it also encompasses decision-making. Using the insights gained from data analysis and pattern recognition, AI systems can make informed decisions about threat prioritization and response strategies. This automated decision-making is particularly crucial in situations where speed is of the essence, such as in real-time threat mitigation.

- **Customization and Contextualization**

A significant advantage of AI in cybersecurity is its ability to customize and contextualize security protocols for different environments. AI systems can learn the specific patterns and behaviors typical in a particular network, allowing for a more tailored security approach. This customization means that the AI system's security measures are not just generic but are finely tuned to the specific needs and vulnerabilities of each environment.

3.4. How AI Enhances Cybersecurity

- **Automated Threat Detection**

First, let's talk about automated threat detection. In simple terms, AI systems are like vigilant guardians that never sleep. They continuously scan the digital landscape to detect anything unusual or potentially harmful. Think of AI as a detective with superhuman abilities to spot clues and patterns that might indicate a cyber threat. This is like having an extra set of eyes that are incredibly sharp, constantly watching over your digital space to catch any bad guys trying to sneak in.

- **Anomaly Detection and Behavior Analysis**

Now, let's explore anomaly detection and behavior analysis. Anomalies are like the odd ones out - things that don't follow the usual pattern. In cybersecurity, these can be signs of a hacker trying to break in. AI is excellent at picking up these anomalies. It learns what normal behavior looks like on your network and then, like a hawk, watches for any behavior that seems out of place. It's akin to noticing someone acting suspiciously in a neighborhood watch - except AI does this in the digital neighborhood of your network.

- **Predictive Analytics for Future Threat Anticipation**

Finally, predictive analytics. This is where AI turns into a fortune teller of sorts, but instead of reading palms, it predicts future cyber threats. By analyzing tons of data and past incidents, AI can forecast potential security breaches before they happen. It's like a weather forecast for cybersecurity, giving you a heads-up about possible storms (cyber threats) on the horizon so you can be prepared and take shelter (strengthen your defenses).

3.5. AI Algorithms and Models in Cybersecurity

I. Neural Networks: Mirroring the human brain's structure, neural networks consist of layers of interconnected nodes processing complex information. Their ability to learn and adapt makes them ideal for identifying subtle patterns and anomalies in network behavior, crucial for detecting sophisticated cyber threats.

II. Decision Trees: This algorithm uses a tree-like model to make decisions, offering a transparent and easily interpretable structure. In cybersecurity, decision trees help categorize various cyber threats based on their characteristics, aiding in swift and accurate threat identification.

III. Signature-based Detection Algorithms: Signature-based detection algorithms are used to identify known threats based on their unique signatures. These algorithms can be used to detect and respond to malware, viruses, and other types of known threats.

IV. Behavioral Analytics Algorithms: Behavioral analytics algorithms are used to build a baseline of normal network behavior and to detect deviations from that baseline that may indicate a cyber-attack. These algorithms can be used to identify insider threats

V. and other malicious activities, as well as to detect and respond to external threats.

VI. Clustering Algorithms: These are essential for grouping large datasets into clusters based on similarity without prior labeling. In the context of cybersecurity, clustering is particularly effective in anomaly detection, as it helps in identifying unusual data patterns that could indicate a breach or an attack.

VII. Support Vector Machines (SVMs): Renowned for their accuracy in classification tasks, SVMs are adept at distinguishing between normal and malicious activities in a network. They work by identifying the optimal boundary (hyperplane) that separates different classes of data, such as benign and malicious network traffic.

3.6. Leveraging Machine Learning Models

1. **Supervised Learning Models:** These models, trained on labeled data, are vital in scenarios where the outcomes are known, such as spam detection. In cybersecurity, they're used to teach systems to recognize known threats effectively.
2. **Unsupervised Learning Models:** Working with unlabeled data, these models excel in discovering hidden patterns and are invaluable in cybersecurity for identifying novel or evolving threats where prior labeling is impossible.
3. **Reinforcement Learning:** This advanced learning method involves models that learn optimal behaviors through trial and error. It's increasingly being applied in cybersecurity to develop systems capable of dynamically adapting their defense mechanisms in response to changing attack strategies.

Training and Testing for Optimal Performance

I. Data Splitting: Critical to the development of robust AI models in cybersecurity is the division of data into training and testing sets. The training set is used to build the model, while the testing set evaluates its effectiveness and accuracy in real-world scenarios.

II. Cross-Validation: This method is crucial for ensuring that AI models in cybersecurity are not just effective for the data they were trained on but can generalize their capabilities to new, unseen data.

III. Fine-Tuning and Optimization: Given the ever-evolving nature of cyber threats, AI models require continuous refinement and optimization to maintain their effectiveness, necessitating regular updates and adjustments based on the latest threat intelligence.

Navigating Challenges

I. Complexity and Interpretability: Some AI models, particularly deep learning networks, can be complex 'black boxes,' making it challenging to understand their decision-making processes. This lack of transparency can be a significant issue in cybersecurity, where understanding the 'why' behind a decision can be as critical as the decision itself.

II. Data Quality and Bias: The efficacy of AI in cybersecurity is heavily reliant on the data it's trained on. Inaccurate or biased data can lead to flawed decision-making, underscoring the importance of high-quality, diverse data sources.

III. Vulnerability to Adversarial Attacks: AI systems are not impervious to attacks. There's a growing concern about adversarial attacks where malicious actors feed deceptive data to AI systems, aiming to confuse and mislead them.

3.7. AI-Driven Security Tools

1. **Enhanced Intrusion Detection Systems (IDS)**: Modern IDS have evolved from traditional, rule-based systems to more dynamic, AI-powered models. These systems excel in detecting anomalies in real time, which is crucial for identifying sophisticated attacks like zero-day exploits and advanced persistent threats. The AI-driven IDS continuously learn from network data, adapting to new threats and reducing false positives, ensuring effectiveness even as cyber threats evolve.
2. **AI in Behavioral Analysis**: The application of AI in monitoring and analyzing user behavior has become a cornerstone in cybersecurity. These tools, by building profiles of normal user behavior, are adept at detecting activities that deviate from established patterns. This is especially useful in identifying potential insider threats or compromised accounts. Predictive behavior modeling offered by these tools acts as an early warning system, enabling a proactive approach to threat detection.
3. **Automated Response Systems:** AI-driven tools are not limited to threat detection; they extend to automating responses to security threats. These systems can take immediate actions, such as isolating affected systems or blocking malicious traffic. Beyond mere automation, they

possess decision-making capabilities to assess threat severity and determine appropriate responses, thereby accelerating threat containment and reducing the workload on human security teams.

4. **Threat Intelligence Platforms:** In the realm of threat intelligence, AI plays a pivotal role. These platforms leverage AI to aggregate and analyze data from various sources, providing comprehensive and contextual insights into the threat landscape. This level of intelligence is crucial for tailoring cybersecurity strategies to specific organizational needs, making threat intelligence more actionable and relevant.
5. **Security Orchestration, Automation, and Response (SOAR):** SOAR platforms embody the integration and automation aspect of AI in cybersecurity. They streamline security operations by coordinating various security tools and automating complex workflows. This orchestration enhances the efficiency and effectiveness of security operations centers (SOCs), making them more responsive to emerging threats.
6. **AI in Vulnerability Management:** AI tools also play a key role in vulnerability management. They proactively identify and assess potential vulnerabilities, prioritizing them based on their impact and exploitability. This predictive capability ensures that remediation efforts are focused on the most critical vulnerabilities, enhancing the security posture of an organization.

How Do These Tools Work?

AI-driven security tools work by analyzing vast amounts of data. They look for patterns, anomalies, or anything that seems out of the ordinary. They're trained on huge datasets, learning from past cyber-attacks to recognize potential future threats. What makes them special is their ability to get smarter over time. They learn from every new piece of data, constantly improving their detection and response capabilities.

Real-World Applications

Let's take a real-world example. Say a company uses an AI-driven security system. One day, this system spots a pattern of data that looks slightly odd. It's not a known virus or a typical cyber-attack pattern, but it's unusual enough to raise a red flag. The system quickly isolates the suspicious data, analyzes it, and realizes it's a new type of malware. It then updates its database and automatically fortifies the network against this new threat. All this happens swiftly, often without any need for human intervention.

Despite their advanced capabilities, AI-driven security tools come with challenges. Their integration into existing infrastructures can be complex, and they require continuous updates and training to stay effective against evolving cyber threats. Additionally, the effectiveness of these tools heavily relies on the quality of the data they process, highlighting the importance of robust data management practices.

3.8. Integrating AI into Existing Security Frameworks

Why Mix AI with Traditional Security?

First off, why do we even want to mix AI with traditional security methods? Imagine you have a guard who's been protecting a fort for years. He's good, but he can't be everywhere at once, right? Now, give him a drone that can fly around, see everything, and learn patterns of what's normal and what's fishy. That's kind of what AI does for cybersecurity. It doesn't replace the guard; it makes him a superhero!

The Challenge of Making Them Work Together

Now, getting AI to work with your existing security isn't just plug-and-play. It's more like adding a new member to a team. Everyone needs to understand each other and work in sync. Here's the tricky part: your current security system might be like an old dog, a bit set in its ways. So, integrating AI is a bit like teaching this old dog some new, high-tech tricks.

Best Practices for Integration

- Start with a Chat: Just like introducing a new teammate, start by figuring out where AI can help the most. Maybe it's sorting through alerts faster or keeping an eye on places that are hard to monitor.
- Slow and Steady: Don't try to overhaul everything overnight.

Start small. Maybe first use AI to analyze logs or monitor network traffic. As it learns and proves itself, it expands its role.

- Training is Key: Just like training a new employee, you need to train your AI. Feed it the right data, show it what normal looks like, and teach it to spot anomalies. It's a learning process for both the AI and your team.
- Teamwork Makes the Dream Work: The goal is for AI and your existing security measures to complement each other. AI can handle the heavy data crunching and pattern recognition while your team focuses on more complex decision-making and strategy.
- Keep an Eye on Things: Just because AI is smart doesn't mean it's always right. Regularly check on what it's doing. Is it flagging the right things? Is it missing anything? Continuous monitoring and adjustment are key.

Real-Life Success Stories

To give you an idea of how this works in the real world, let's look at a couple of examples. Some companies have successfully integrated AI to automatically detect and respond to threats faster than any human could. Others use AI to predict where attacks might come from, kind of like a weather forecast for cyber threats!

CHAPTER 4: TECHNOLOGIES BEHIND SELF-DEFENDING NETWORKS

4.1. INTRODUCTION

Security is one of the fastest-growing areas in the networking and IT industries today. Security is often the top concern of Chief Information Officers (CIOs) and one of the top technology initiatives of many organizations. However, security projects often do not get the focus needed to be approved and deployed. Perhaps this reticence can be explained by the complexity of security. Cisco has reduced the cost of deploying and managing security by creating a self-defending network. The self-defending network can enable the network to detect and defend itself against certain attacks.

Self-defending networks represent a paradigm shift in cybersecurity. Traditionally, network security has been reactive, often relying on human intervention to identify and respond to threats. This approach, while effective to a degree, has limitations, especially in the face of increasingly sophisticated cyber-attacks. Self-defending networks, on the other hand, are designed to be proactive, utilizing a combination of advanced technologies to autonomously detect, prevent, and mitigate threats.

The core idea of a self-defending network is to create a system that is not only aware of its environment but can also adapt and respond in real-time to potential threats. This approach significantly reduces the time between the detection of a threat and its mitigation, a crucial factor in minimizing the impact of cyber-attacks. The importance of self-defending networks is underscored by the exponential increase in both the volume and complexity of cyber threats in recent years. These networks are not just an advancement in technology; they are a necessary evolution in the face of the ever-evolving cyber threat landscape.

The Shift from Traditional Security Approaches

Traditional network security systems are based on predefined rules and known threat signatures. They rely heavily on firewalls, antivirus software, and intrusion detection systems, which are adept at handling known threats but often fall short when encountering new or evolving threats. Moreover, the increasing complexity of networks, with the integration of cloud computing, Internet of Things (IoT) devices, and remote access, has exposed new vulnerabilities that traditional systems struggle to address.

Self-defending networks address these challenges by incorporating advanced technologies such as artificial intelligence (AI), machine learning (ML), and behavioral analytics. These technologies enable the network to learn and adapt continuously, identifying and responding to threats based on behavior patterns and anomaly detection rather than relying solely on known threat signatures.

AI and ML algorithms can analyze vast amounts of network data in real time, identifying even the subtlest deviations from normal behavior that may indicate a security breach. This capability is crucial in detecting zero-day exploits and advanced persistent threats (APTs), which are designed to evade traditional security measures.

Behavioral analytics further enhances this capability by providing a deeper understanding of the network's typical behavior. By establishing a baseline of normal activities, the system can more accurately identify anomalous and potentially malicious behavior. This approach is particularly effective in detecting insider threats and sophisticated attacks that mimic legitimate activities.

The shift to self-defending networks is not just about adopting new technologies but also involves a fundamental change in the approach to cybersecurity. It requires building security into the network's architecture, ensuring that every component, from endpoints to data centers, is an active participant in the defense strategy. This integrated approach ensures a more robust and resilient network capable of defending itself against the sophisticated threats of the digital age.

4.2. INTRODUCING TO ML and AI in Cybersecurity

In the realm of cybersecurity, Machine Learning (ML) and Artificial Intelligence (AI) are transformative technologies that empower computers to learn from data, recognize patterns, and make intelligent decisions with minimal human intervention. These technologies have become pivotal in identifying cyber threats, predicting potential attacks, and automating complex decision-making processes that are crucial for modern network security.

ML and AI algorithms analyze data at a scale and speed beyond human capability. They scrutinize network traffic, user behavior, and system activities, learning to distinguish between normal operations and potential security threats. This ability is particularly vital in an era where the volume, variety, and velocity of data overwhelm traditional security measures.

Evolution of AI in Cybersecurity

The evolution of AI in cybersecurity is a journey from rudimentary rule-based systems to sophisticated neural network-driven solutions. Initially, cybersecurity relied heavily on static rule-based algorithms. These systems, governed by predefined rules, were effective against known threats but struggled with new or evolving attacks.

As cyber threats grew more complex and elusive, the need for adaptive and intelligent security systems became apparent. This need led to the integration of ML and AI in cybersecurity.

I. From Rule-Based to Learning Algorithms: The shift began with the adoption of machine learning models that could learn from data, identify patterns, and make decisions. Unlike rule-based systems, ML algorithms adapt to new information, making them more effective against unknown threats.
II. Rise of Neural Networks and Deep Learning: The advent of neural networks and deep learning marked a significant milestone. These advanced AI models, inspired by the human brain's structure and function, excel in identifying intricate patterns and making complex decisions. Deep learning algorithms are particularly effective in processing unstructured data, such as images and natural language, opening new frontiers in threat detection and analysis.
III. Sophistication in Threat Detection: Modern AI systems in cybersecurity use sophisticated algorithms to analyze not just malware signatures but also behavioral patterns and anomalies that indicate a breach. This shift from signature-based to behavior-based detection is pivotal in countering zero-day attacks and advanced persistent threats (APTs).
IV. Automation and Autonomous Response: The latest AI advancements have enabled the development of autonomous security systems. These systems not only detect threats but also respond to them in real-time, often without the need for human intervention. This autonomy is critical in managing the scale and sophistication of modern cyber threats.

The role of ML and AI in cybersecurity is multifaceted:

I. Pattern Recognition: These systems excel in identifying patterns and anomalies within large datasets, enabling early detection of malware, intrusions, and suspicious activities.

II. Threat Prediction: By analyzing historical data and current trends, AI algorithms can predict and anticipate future attack strategies, allowing for preemptive measures.

III. Automated Decision-Making: In fast-paced cyber environments, AI-driven systems make rapid and accurate decisions about threat containment and response, reducing the window of vulnerability.

Types of Machine Learning Algorithms in Cybersecurity

Machine learning (ML) in cybersecurity utilizes various algorithm types, each serving unique functions in protecting networks against diverse threats.

- Supervised Learning

Supervised learning algorithms, trained on labeled datasets, excel in recognizing known threats like malware and phishing attacks. These models compare incoming data against known threat signatures to identify potential risks. For instance, they analyze characteristics of phishing emails—like misleading links or deceptive language—to effectively spot similar future attempts.

- Unsupervised Learning

Unsupervised learning, on the other hand, is pivotal for identifying unknown or emerging threats. These algorithms analyze network traffic and user behavior to establish a baseline of normal activities. Any deviation from this baseline, such as unusual data movement or login patterns, could indicate a security breach. This approach is particularly effective in detecting sophisticated attacks like zero-day exploits, which are not identified by traditional signature-based methods.

- Reinforcement Learning

Reinforcement learning, a more dynamic approach, adapts by learning from the environment. In cybersecurity, these algorithms continuously refine their decision-making strategies based on the outcomes of previous actions. This adaptability is crucial for developing advanced threat response systems that can autonomously adjust their tactics in real-time, countering threats as they evolve.

Application of AI in Network Security

The application of Artificial Intelligence (AI) in network security represents a paradigm shift in how cyber threats are identified, analyzed, and mitigated. AI's integration into network security brings a level of sophistication and efficiency that is essential in the face of evolving and increasingly complex cyber threats. This comprehensive examination highlights the multifaceted role of AI in enhancing network security.

- Revolutionizing Threat Detection and Response

AI systems, with their ability to analyze vast amounts of data and learn from it, have significantly advanced threat detection. Unlike traditional methods that rely on recognizing known malware signatures, AI-driven systems use machine learning algorithms to detect anomalies and patterns indicative of novel or evolving cyber threats. This capability is crucial for identifying zero-day vulnerabilities and sophisticated malware that would evade traditional security measures.

These AI systems are not limited to passive monitoring; they actively predict potential security incidents by analyzing data trends and patterns. This predictive approach enables network administrators to proactively address vulnerabilities, fortify defenses, and mitigate risks before they are exploited.

- Automating Incident Response

In the event of a security breach, the speed and accuracy of the response are critical. AI-driven systems excel in this aspect by automating responses to detected threats. This automation ranges from isolating affected systems to deploying patches and alerting stakeholders, significantly reducing the window of opportunity for attackers to cause damage.

- Enhancing Threat Intelligence Integration

AI enhances the capacity to aggregate and interpret threat intelligence from diverse sources, offering a more comprehensive view of the threat landscape. This integration facilitates informed decision-making and strategy development, adapting dynamically as new data emerges. The result is a security posture that is not only reactive but also anticipatory, adapting to new threats as they arise.

- Optimizing Security Protocols and Compliance

AI technologies are instrumental in continuously updating and optimizing security protocols to ensure they remain effective against current threats. This includes adaptive firewalls, intrusion detection systems, and endpoint security solutions. Moreover, AI aids in ensuring compliance with cybersecurity regulations by automating the monitoring and reporting processes, thus simplifying the management of compliance requirements.

- User Behavior Analysis and Insider Threat Detection

A critical aspect of AI in network security is its ability to analyze user behavior to detect insider threats. By monitoring user activities and identifying deviations from normal patterns, AI systems can alert administrators to potential security breaches from within the organization, an area traditionally challenging to secure.

Enhancing Decision-Making with AI in Network Security

- Data Analysis and Interpretation

I. Understanding Complex Data: AI excels at interpreting complex and voluminous data that would be overwhelming for humans. Cybersecurity generates enormous amounts of data, including logs, network traffic, and user behavior. AI algorithms can sift through this data rapidly, identifying important patterns and anomalies.

II. Real-Time Analysis: AI systems analyze data in real-time, providing immediate insights. This is crucial in cybersecurity, where threats can emerge and escalate quickly. Real-time analysis helps in promptly identifying and mitigating potential security breaches.

III. Enhanced Pattern Recognition: AI uses sophisticated algorithms to recognize patterns that might indicate a cyber threat. These patterns could be unusual network traffic, unexpected system behavior, or known signatures of malware. AI's ability to detect these patterns, often invisible to the human eye, is a significant asset in preemptive threat detection.

- Risk Assessment and Management

I. Evaluating Threats: AI systems assess the risk level of identified threats by considering various factors like the nature of the threat, affected systems, and potential impact. This helps in prioritizing responses and allocating resources more effectively.

II. Predictive Risk Analysis: AI goes beyond current data,

utilizing machine learning to predict future security risks. By analyzing trends and historical data, AI can forecast potential vulnerabilities and advise on preemptive measures, reducing the likelihood of future attacks.

III. Decision Support for Security Teams: AI provides valuable insights and recommendations to security teams, aiding in decision-making. It presents complex data in a more understandable format, making it easier for teams to make informed decisions quickly.

- <u>Automated Incident Response</u>

I. Automating Responses: In the event of a security breach, time is of the essence. AI-driven systems can automatically initiate responses to mitigate threats, such as isolating affected systems, blocking malicious traffic, or deploying patches.

II. Dynamic Adaptation: AI systems adapt their response strategies based on the nature of the threat. This dynamic adaptation ensures that the response is not only swift but also appropriate to the specific type of attack.

III. Learning from Incidents: Post-incident, AI systems can analyze what happened and learn from it. This continuous learning process enhances the system's ability to respond to similar threats in the future.

Challenges and Considerations

I. Balancing Automation and Human Oversight: While AI can automate many decision-making processes, the importance of human oversight cannot be understated. Decisions regarding complex and high-stakes threats often require human judgment and expertise.

II. Ethical and Privacy Concerns: The use of AI in decision-making raises ethical questions, particularly about privacy. It's essential to ensure that AI systems respect user privacy and comply with relevant regulations.

III. Avoiding Overreliance: There's a risk of becoming overly reliant on AI, which might lead to complacency in security practices. A balanced approach, combining AI's capabilities with human expertise, is crucial.

Integration Challenges and Solutions

- Data Quality and Availability

Challenge: ML and AI models are only as good as the data they are trained on. High-quality, relevant, and comprehensive data is essential for these models to effectively learn and make accurate predictions. However, acquiring such datasets can be challenging due to privacy concerns, data sensitivity, and the sheer volume of data required.

Solution:

I. Data Anonymization and Synthesis: Implementing data anonymization techniques to protect sensitive information while using it for training purposes. Synthetic data generation can also supplement real-world data, providing diverse scenarios for model training.

II. Data Sharing Initiatives: Collaborating within the cybersecurity community to share threat intelligence and data. This collective approach can enrich training datasets and enhance the overall effectiveness of AI models.

- Algorithmic Bias and Ethical Considerations

Challenge: AI algorithms can inherit biases present in their training data, leading to skewed or unfair outcomes. In cybersecurity, this bias might manifest as higher false positive rates for certain types of network traffic or users. Additionally, there are ethical concerns regarding privacy and the autonomous nature of decision-making in AI systems.

Solution:

I. Diverse Training Data: Ensuring that training datasets are diverse and representative of different scenarios to minimize bias.
II. Ethical AI Frameworks: Developing and adhering to ethical guidelines for AI in cybersecurity, focusing on transparency, accountability, and fairness.
III. Regular Audits and Updates: Conduct periodic audits of AI systems to identify and correct biases and update models regularly to adapt to new data and contexts.

- Continual Learning and Adaptation

Challenge: The cybersecurity landscape is constantly evolving, with new threats emerging regularly. ML and AI models need to continually learn and adapt to these changes to remain effective.

Solution:

I. Adaptive Learning Algorithms: Implementing machine learning algorithms capable of continual learning and adaptation. These algorithms can update their knowledge base without being explicitly reprogrammed.
II. Feedback Loops: Establishing feedback mechanisms where AI systems learn from their successes and failures, incorporating this learning into future operations.

- Balancing Security with Usability and Privacy

Challenge: Implementing robust AI-driven security measures can sometimes conflict with user privacy and system usability. Overly aggressive security protocols might impede legitimate network activities or infringe on user privacy.

Solution:

I. User-Centric Design: Designing AI systems with a focus on user experience, ensuring that security measures do not overly burden legitimate users.
II. Privacy-Preserving Technologies: Leveraging technologies like homomorphic encryption and differential privacy to analyze data while preserving user privacy.
III. Customizable Security Policies: Allowing for customizable security settings that can be tailored to balance the needs of security, privacy, and usability for different environments.

Future Directions in AI for Cybersecurity

The landscape of AI in cybersecurity is rapidly evolving, driven by the relentless advancement of technology and the ever-changing nature of cyber threats. As we look to the future, several key areas are poised to redefine how AI will further enhance cybersecurity measures.

- Advanced Neural Networks and Deep Learning

Neural Network Complexity: Future AI systems in cybersecurity are likely to leverage more complex and sophisticated neural network architectures. These advanced networks can process and analyze data with unprecedented depth, allowing for a more nuanced understanding and prediction of cyber threats.

Deep Learning Applications: Deep learning, a subset of machine learning based on artificial neural networks, is expected to play a significant role in detecting sophisticated cyber threats. With its ability to learn from vast amounts of unstructured data, deep learning can uncover subtle patterns indicative of advanced persistent threats and zero-day exploits.

- AI and Quantum Computing

Quantum-Enhanced Cybersecurity: The advent of quantum computing presents both a challenge and an opportunity for AI in cybersecurity. Quantum computers could potentially break current encryption methods, but they also offer a new frontier for AI algorithms. Quantum-enhanced AI could process information at unprecedented speeds, leading to more efficient threat detection and response systems.

- Predictive Cybersecurity

Predictive Analytics: AI's capability to analyze trends and predict future patterns will become more refined. Predictive cybersecurity, powered by AI, will proactively identify potential vulnerabilities and threats before they are exploited, shifting the paradigm from reactive to preemptive security measures.

- Autonomous Response and Decision-Making

- Automated Incident Response: AI systems will advance towards more autonomous response capabilities. These systems will not only detect threats but also execute sophisticated response strategies without human intervention, reducing response times and mitigating the impact of attacks.
- Decision-Making AI: As AI systems become more capable, they will play a significant role in decision-making processes in cybersecurity. This includes evaluating the severity of threats, prioritizing responses, and even making strategic security decisions.

Cross-Domain AI Applications

Interdisciplinary Approaches: The future of AI in cybersecurity will likely see a convergence with AI advancements in other fields. Techniques developed in areas like natural language processing, computer vision, and behavioral analysis could find novel applications in cybersecurity, offering innovative ways to tackle complex security challenges.

Ethical AI and Bias Mitigation

- Ethical Considerations: As AI takes on more significant roles in cybersecurity, ethical considerations will become increasingly important. Ensuring that AI systems are transparent, accountable, and free from biases will be crucial in maintaining trust and effectiveness.
- Bias Detection and Correction: AI systems must be designed to identify and correct their biases, particularly in the context of threat detection and response. This is vital to avoid false positives and ensure equitable and accurate security measures across different systems and users.

Collaborative AI and Crowdsourcing

- Collaborative AI Systems: The future may see the development of collaborative AI systems where multiple AI agents work together, sharing insights and learning from each other. This collaborative approach can enhance the overall effectiveness and adaptability of cybersecurity strategies.
- Crowdsourcing for AI Training: Leveraging crowdsourcing for gathering data and training AI models can lead to more robust and comprehensive cybersecurity solutions. This approach can help AI systems learn from a diverse range of scenarios and threats, enhancing their ability to generalize and

adapt.

4.3. Behavioral Analytics and Anomaly Detection

Behavioral Analytics: The Foundation of Modern Network Security

Behavioral analytics stands as a pivotal innovation, fundamentally reshaping how network security is approached and managed. This advanced technology delves deep into the analysis of user and network behavior patterns, offering a proactive and adaptive means of defending against cyber threats.

At its core, behavioral analytics begins by mapping out a baseline of what constitutes 'normal' activity within a network. This baseline encompasses a range of user behaviors and network interactions, from typical login times and data transfer volumes to routine resource access patterns. Unlike static security systems, behavioral analytics is characterized by its dynamic nature, constantly monitoring network activities and evolving with each new piece of data. This ongoing process of learning and adaptation is key to its effectiveness, allowing the system to stay in step with the ever-changing landscape of network usage and potential threats.

One of the standout capabilities of behavioral analytics is its nuanced approach to anomaly detection. By understanding the intricacies of network and user behavior, it can pinpoint anomalies that might be overlooked by traditional security measures. Whether it's irregular access to sensitive data or an uncharacteristic spike in data transfer, behavioral analytics discerns these irregularities with precision, significantly reducing the occurrence of false positives. This accuracy is crucial not only for identifying genuine threats but also for minimizing unnecessary alarms that could burden security teams.

Beyond mere detection, behavioral analytics also brings predictive power to the table. By analyzing trends and patterns, it can forecast potential security incidents, offering a chance to preempt and neutralize threats before they manifest into full-blown attacks. This forward-looking capability marks a shift from reactive to predictive security management, a vital transition in an era where cyber threats are increasingly sophisticated and elusive.

The adaptability of behavioral analytics is particularly relevant in the context of emerging threats. As attackers evolve their tactics, so does the analytics system, ensuring that network defenses remain robust and effective. In many cutting-edge implementations, this technology is equipped with automated response mechanisms. These systems can act immediately upon detecting a potential threat, curtailing the window of opportunity for attackers and mitigating risks in real-time.

Behavioral analytics also extends its reach beyond traditional users to include all entities within the network, such as devices and applications. This comprehensive approach, often referred to as User and Entity Behavior Analytics (UEBA), ensures a more all-encompassing security posture, protecting against both external threats and potential insider risks.

When integrated into the broader security ecosystem, including solutions like SIEMs and intrusion detection systems, behavioral analytics enhances the overall security posture of a network. It offers a nuanced view of the security landscape, enabling more informed and coordinated responses to threats. This integration is a testament to the technology's role not just as a standalone tool but as a critical component in a multifaceted defense strategy.

Anomaly Detection: The AI-Driven Sentinel in Network Security

Anomaly detection stands as a critical component in the architecture of self-defending networks, leveraging AI to identify unusual patterns that could indicate security threats. This process is essential in modern cybersecurity for several reasons:

1. Sophisticated Machine Learning Models: At the core of anomaly detection are advanced machine learning models. These models are trained on vast datasets to understand what normal network behavior looks like. Once trained, they can effortlessly identify deviations that might signify a cyber-attack or system vulnerability. The use of varied algorithms, including neural networks, statistical analysis, and pattern recognition, allows these systems to continuously learn and improve their detection capabilities.
2. Real-time Surveillance and Rapid Response: Anomaly detection operates in real-time, continuously analyzing network traffic and activities. This ongoing surveillance enables immediate identification of potential threats, allowing for swift responses to mitigate risks. In a landscape where cyber threats evolve rapidly; this real-time analysis is crucial for maintaining network integrity and security.
3. Dynamic Baseline Establishment: Unlike traditional methods that rely on static thresholds for detecting anomalies, modern AI-driven systems dynamically adjust their baseline definitions of "normal" behavior. This continuous adjustment accounts for legitimate changes in network activity, thus reducing false positives while enhancing detection accuracy. By understanding the fluid nature of network traffic, these systems ensure that only genuine anomalies that pose potential threats are flagged.

4. Comprehensive Threat Analysis: Anomaly detection is most effective when integrated with a broader security framework. By correlating data from various sources, such as user activities, application logs, and network traffic, these systems provide a holistic view of the security landscape. This comprehensive analysis helps in distinguishing between benign anomalies and actual security threats.
5. Proactive Threat Prediction: Leveraging predictive analytics, anomaly detection systems can forecast potential security incidents before they occur. By analyzing emerging patterns and comparing them with known threat behaviors, these systems can alert administrators to potential risks, allowing preemptive action to avert potential breaches.

4.4. Encryption and Cryptography

Encryption: Encryption is a process of converting data or information into a code to prevent unauthorized access. This transformation involves using an algorithm known as a cipher and a key to turn the original readable data, known as plaintext, into an unreadable format called ciphertext. The key is a secret parameter that determines the output of the encryption process. Encryption ensures that even if data is intercepted during transmission or storage, it remains confidential and inaccessible to unauthorized entities. There are two main types of encryption: symmetric, where the same key is used for both encrypting and decrypting the data, and asymmetric, which uses a pair of keys – one public and one private – for enhanced security.

Cryptography: Cryptography is the science and practice of designing secure communication systems that protect information from adversaries. It encompasses a broad range of practices and techniques, including encryption, decryption, and various methods of safeguarding data integrity, authentication, and non-repudiation. Cryptography not only involves the development of methods to securely encrypt and decrypt data but also involves the creation and analysis of protocols that prevent third parties or the public from reading private messages. Modern cryptography intersects with disciplines such as mathematics, computer science, and electrical engineering and plays a critical role in securing digital communications and information in various fields such as finance, government, and healthcare.

The Role of Encryption

1. Data Protection: Encryption transforms readable data into a coded format that can only be deciphered with a specific key. In the context of self-defending networks, this means that even if attackers manage to infiltrate the network, the data they access will be unintelligible and useless without the decryption keys.
2. Secure Communication: Encryption ensures that the data transmitted across the network remains secure. This is crucial for remote access, cloud computing, and IoT devices that constantly send and receive data across potentially insecure networks.
3. Compliance and Trust: Many industries have strict regulatory requirements for data protection, such as GDPR or HIPAA. Employing robust encryption methods helps organizations meet these compliance requirements and builds trust with customers and partners.

Advances in Cryptographic Techniques

1. Symmetric vs. Asymmetric Encryption: Symmetric encryption uses the same key for both encryption and decryption, making it faster but less versatile. Asymmetric encryption, on the other hand, uses a pair of keys (public and private) and is essential for secure internet communications, like SSL/TLS for web transactions.
2. Quantum Cryptography: With the advent of quantum computing, traditional encryption methods face the risk of becoming obsolete. Quantum cryptography, however, uses the principles of quantum mechanics, providing a level of security that is theoretically immune to quantum computer attacks.
3. Homomorphic Encryption: This revolutionary technique allows computations to be performed on encrypted data without needing to decrypt it first. It holds immense potential for privacy-preserving data analysis, particularly in cloud computing environments.

Integration of Encryption and Cryptography in Self-Defending Networks

1. Automated Key Management: Self-defending networks automate the process of generating, rotating, distributing, and storing encryption keys. This automation minimizes the risk of key compromise and ensures that encryption practices adhere to security standards.

2. Adaptive Encryption Strategies: These networks use AI algorithms to analyze network traffic and threat levels, adjusting encryption methods in real time. This adaptive approach allows for context-aware encryption, applying

stronger encryption for sensitive data and lighter encryption for less critical information, thus balancing security with network performance.

3. Securing Data in Transit and At Rest: All data moving across the network is protected with end-to-end encryption, especially in untrusted environments, to prevent interception and eavesdropping. Similarly, sensitive data stored within the network is encrypted to safeguard against unauthorized access or data breaches.

4. IoT Security: In the realm of IoT, self-defending networks ensure device-level encryption and employ cryptographic methods for secure device authentication. This is crucial for maintaining the integrity of data from IoT devices as they interact with the network.

5. Blockchain Integration: Blockchain technology is used to create a tamper-proof ledger for sensitive transactions, enhancing data integrity. Smart contracts on blockchain can automate and enforce security policies, adding an extra layer of security.

Challenges and Considerations

I. Performance Overheads: Encryption can introduce latency and performance overheads. Balancing the level of encryption with network performance is crucial, especially in time-sensitive environments.
II. Key Management Complexities: Effective key management is critical but complex. Poorly managed keys can become a security liability.
III. Evolving Threat Landscape: As cryptographic techniques

evolve, so do the methods used by cybercriminals. Ongoing research and development are vital to stay ahead of threats.

4.5. Automated Threat Intelligence and Response Systems

Automated Threat Intelligence and Response Systems represent a transformative approach in cybersecurity, leveraging automation and advanced analytics to proactively identify, assess, and neutralize cyber threats. These systems are integral to self-defending networks, providing them with the agility and intelligence necessary to respond to an ever-evolving threat landscape.

Key Components of Automated Threat Intelligence and Response Systems

- Data-Driven Threat Intelligence

I. Data Collection: This involves aggregating vast amounts of data from diverse sources, including network logs, real-time traffic, external threat databases, and past incident reports. The system must be equipped to handle structured and unstructured data, ensuring a comprehensive view of potential threats.

II. Intelligence Analysis: Leveraging advanced machine learning algorithms, the system sifts through this data to identify patterns, anomalies, and potential indicators of compromise. This process is not just about volume but also about the sophistication in discerning relevant threat indicators from benign anomalies.

- Real-Time Analysis and Automated Decision-Making

I. Contextual Analysis: The system must interpret data in the context of the network's normal behavior, considering factors like time, location, user behavior, and network traffic patterns. This context is crucial for accurately identifying genuine threats.
II. Automated Decision-Making: Once a potential threat is identified, the system must decide on the appropriate course of action. This involves distinguishing between false positives and genuine threats, prioritizing them based on potential impact, and initiating responses without the need for human intervention.

- Automated Response and Mitigation

I. Predefined Response Protocols: The system should have a range of response protocols tailored to different types of threats. These can include isolating infected systems, blocking malicious traffic, or deploying patches.
II. Dynamic Response Adaptation: In addition to predefined responses, the system should be capable of adapting its response strategies in real-time based on the nature and severity of the attack. This adaptability ensures that the network can defend against novel or evolving threats.

Adaptive Learning and Continuous Improvement

1. Feedback Loop: A critical component is the feedback loop, where the system learns from each incident. By analyzing the outcomes of its responses, the system can continuously refine

its detection models and response strategies.

2. Continuous Learning: The system should not only learn from its own experiences but also integrate new threat intelligence from external sources. This continuous learning ensures that the system remains up-to-date with the latest threat landscape and is prepared for emerging cyber threats.

Functionality and Benefits

Automated Threat Intelligence and Response Systems stand as critical sentinels, endowed with the capability to not only detect but also counteract cyber threats with remarkable efficiency. These systems, ingrained with sophisticated artificial intelligence, serve as the nerve center of self-defending networks, constantly vigilant and ready to act against potential security breaches.

The primary functionality of these systems lies in their relentless gathering and analysis of threat intelligence. They continuously ingest a vast array of data from diverse sources, including network traffic, system logs, and external threat databases. This information is then meticulously sifted through using advanced machine learning algorithms, enabling the identification of suspicious patterns and indicators of compromise. This process, far beyond the scope of manual analysis, allows for the detection of even the most subtle anomalies that might elude traditional security measures.

Once a potential threat is identified, the true prowess of these systems comes to the fore. Equipped with real-time analysis capabilities, they rapidly assess the threat level, differentiating between false positives and genuine threats. This swift decision-making process is crucial in a landscape where even a few seconds delay can lead to catastrophic data breaches.

The automated response mechanisms these systems deploy are equally impressive. Upon recognizing a threat, predefined response protocols are immediately activated, tailored to counter specific types of attacks. This automation extends to adapting response strategies in real-time, depending on the nature and severity of the attack, ensuring that the network's defenses are not just reactive but also proactive and dynamic.

However, what truly sets these systems apart is their ability to learn and evolve. Every incident, whether a thwarted attack or a false alarm, feeds into a continuous learning process. This feedback loop is invaluable, constantly refining both the threat detection models and the response strategies. Over time, the system becomes increasingly adept at predicting and preemptively neutralizing threats, often before they can manifest into actual attacks.

The benefits of deploying such advanced systems in network security are manifold. Their high-speed analysis and automated responses significantly reduce the time between the detection of a threat and its mitigation, a critical factor in minimizing potential damage. This speed and efficiency are paramount in an era where cyber threats are not only growing in number but also in sophistication.

Furthermore, the predictive capabilities of these systems cannot be understated. By analyzing trends and historical data, they can foresee potential future threats, enabling organizations to implement proactive defenses. This foresight is a game-changer, shifting the paradigm from a reactive to a preventive approach in cybersecurity.

Scalability and adaptability are other key advantages. These systems can handle vast volumes of data and are customizable to various network environments, making them suitable for organizations of all sizes and sectors. By being adaptable, they ensure that the security measures remain robust regardless of the evolving network infrastructure and threat landscape.

Lastly, the reduction in human error is a significant benefit. While human expertise is indispensable, the reliance on automated systems for routine threat detection and response minimizes the chances of oversights and errors. It also allows cybersecurity professionals to focus their skills on more complex and strategic aspects of network security.

Challenges and Considerations

1. Complexity in Implementation and Integration

Implementing automated threat intelligence and response systems is a complex endeavor. These systems must seamlessly integrate with existing security infrastructures, which can vary widely in terms of technology and architecture. Ensuring compatibility and efficient communication between different components can be challenging. Additionally, setting up these systems requires in-depth technical expertise to fine-tune the algorithms and response protocols, ensuring they are tailored to the specific environment and threat landscape of the organization.

2. Reliance on Quality and Completeness of Data

The effectiveness of automated systems is heavily dependent on the quality and completeness of the data they process. Inaccurate, outdated, or incomplete data can lead to incorrect threat assessments, resulting in false positives or, more critically, false negatives. Ensuring a continuous influx of up-to-date and comprehensive threat intelligence is essential. This includes keeping abreast of the latest cyber threat trends, tactics, and techniques used by adversaries.

3. Balancing Automation with Human Oversight

While automation offers speed and efficiency, it's crucial to maintain a balance between automated responses and human oversight. Over-reliance on automation can lead to unintended consequences, such as the accidental blocking of legitimate network traffic or the failure to recognize complex, multi-faceted attack patterns. Periodic human review is essential to validate and adjust automated decisions, ensuring that the system's responses are accurate and appropriate for the evolving threat landscape.

4. Ethical and Privacy Concerns

Automated systems often require access to vast amounts of data, some of which may be sensitive or personal. Ensuring privacy and adhering to ethical standards are paramount. This includes complying with data protection regulations such as GDPR and maintaining transparency in how data is collected, used, and stored. Organizations must also be wary of biases in AI algorithms, which can lead to skewed or unfair outcomes.

5. Continual Adaptation to Evolving Threats

Cyber threats are constantly evolving, with attackers frequently developing new methods to evade detection. Automated systems must, therefore, be designed for continual learning and adaptation. This involves regularly updating algorithms and response strategies based on the latest threat intelligence and feedback from past incidents. The challenge is to stay one step ahead of attackers in an ever-changing cybersecurity landscape.

6. Scalability and Performance Under Pressure

These systems must be scalable to handle the increasing volume and sophistication of cyber-attacks. This includes the ability to process and analyze large datasets quickly and efficiently. During peak times of network activity or during sophisticated, multi-vector attacks, the system's performance must remain robust, ensuring that threat detection and response are not compromised.

4.6. Blockchain for Network Security

Blockchain technology is a form of distributed ledger technology (DLT). At its most basic level, a blockchain is a chain of blocks, where each block contains a number of transactions. Every time a new transaction occurs on the blockchain, a record of that transaction is added to every participant's ledger. This decentralized database, managed by multiple participants, is known as a Distributed Ledger.

A key element of blockchain is that it is not stored in a single location or controlled by a single entity. This distributed nature makes it inherently resistant to the modification of the data. Once recorded, the data in any given block cannot be altered retroactively without altering all subsequent blocks, which requires network consensus.

Key Features Relevant to Cybersecurity

1. **Decentralization:** Unlike traditional centralized networks, where a central authority has control over the entire system, blockchain operates on a peer-to-peer basis. This decentralization is crucial in cybersecurity as it removes single points of failure. If one node is compromised, it does not affect the integrity of the entire network, thus providing a more resilient framework for secure data management.
2. **Immutability:** Each block in a blockchain is linked to the previous block through cryptographic hashes, which are unique identifiers. If any data in a block is altered, its hash

changes completely, making tampering evident. This immutability ensures data integrity and provides a secure and unalterable record of transactions, which is essential for trust in digital interactions.

3. **Transparency:** Blockchain provides a transparent transaction ledger. While user identities are protected by pseudonyms, their transaction history is open and verifiable. This transparency is vital for auditability and traceability in cybersecurity contexts. It allows for easy tracking of data origins and changes, which is crucial in identifying and understanding the nature of cyber threats.

Enhancing Network Security with Blockchain

Blockchain's inherent characteristics significantly bolster network security in several ways:

> Decentralization as Defense: In a decentralized blockchain network, there is no central point of control. This aspect is particularly beneficial for network security as it reduces the risk of central points of failure, which are vulnerable in traditional centralized systems. Cyber attackers cannot compromise the entire network by targeting a single central server, making blockchain-based systems inherently more secure against certain types of cyberattacks, including Distributed Denial of Service (DDoS) attacks.

> Immutability for Data Integrity: The immutability of blockchain ensures that once data is entered, it cannot be altered, providing a secure and trustworthy record of transactions. This feature is essential in cybersecurity to maintain the integrity of data. It is particularly useful in scenarios like tracking the source of a cyberattack, as the

transaction records are tamper-proof and provide a reliable audit trail.

> Transparency and Trust: The transparent nature of blockchain, while maintaining user anonymity, provides a level of trust and traceability that is not available in traditional systems. This transparency enables network participants to verify and audit transactions independently and in real-time. It's especially beneficial in cybersecurity for validating transactions and ensuring that data has not been tampered with.

Use Cases of Blockchain in Network Security

◈ Secure Communication Protocols

Blockchain offers a revolutionary approach to securing digital communications. By treating each message or data transfer as a transaction, blockchain can create highly secure, encrypted messaging systems. This decentralized and encrypted approach ensures that communications are protected against eavesdropping and unauthorized access. Such secure channels are vital in high-stakes environments like military operations, corporate data exchanges, and government communications.

◈ Identity and Access Management (IAM)

Blockchain's application in Identity and Access Management (IAM) introduces a decentralized and secure method for managing digital identities. This technology allows the creation of an immutable digital identity, enhancing the security and integrity of user verification processes. By giving users control over their identity data, blockchain-based IAM systems enhance privacy and security, making them ideal for use in industries like healthcare, financial services, and government sectors, where strict access control is paramount.

◈ Secure DNS and DDoS Protection

In addressing the vulnerabilities of traditional DNS systems, blockchain offers a decentralized solution that significantly reduces risks like cache poisoning and DDoS attacks. By distributing DNS entries across a network of nodes, blockchain makes DNS tampering and DDoS attacks much more challenging. This increased security and resilience are crucial for critical infrastructure and online services that demand high availability and robust defense against cyber-attacks.

◈ Blockchain-Enabled Threat Intelligence Sharing

Blockchain enables secure and anonymous platforms for sharing cyber threat intelligence. Organizations can contribute to and access a shared ledger of threat data and Indicators of Compromise (IoCs) without compromising sensitive information. This collective intelligence approach allows organizations to gain a more comprehensive understanding of cyber threats, enhancing their defensive capabilities. The creation of a decentralized, tamper-proof repository for threat data using blockchain is especially valuable for sectors frequently targeted by cybercriminals, such as the financial industry and government agencies.

Addressing IoT Security Challenges with Blockchain

1. Enhancing Device Identity Management

Traditional IoT systems often struggle with securely identifying and authenticating devices. Blockchain can provide a decentralized and tamper-proof registry for IoT devices, ensuring each device has a unique, verifiable identity. This can prevent unauthorized devices from accessing the network.

2. Securing Firmware Updates

Firmware updates are critical for IoT security but are vulnerable to tampering. Blockchain can be used to verify the authenticity and integrity of firmware updates. By recording firmware updates on a blockchain, it becomes easier to ensure that the updates are not altered during transmission.

3. Maintaining Data Integrity

IoT devices generate vast amounts of data, which can be vulnerable to manipulation. Blockchain ensures the integrity of this data by creating an immutable record. This can be crucial in applications where data authenticity is paramount, such as in healthcare or industrial IoT.

Examples of Blockchain Integration in IoT Networks

4. Smart homes: Using blockchain to manage and secure the multitude of IoT devices in a smart home environment.

1. Supply chain: Blockchain for tracking and securing the flow of goods and information in IoT-enabled supply chains.
2. Health monitoring systems: Using blockchain to securely store and manage patient data collected by IoT health monitoring devices.

Utilizing Smart Contracts for Automating Security Responses

� Automated Policy Enforcement

Smart contracts can automatically enforce security policies in a network. For example, if an IoT device behaves anomalously, a smart contract can automatically isolate the device or restrict its access based on predefined rules.

� Real-time Threat Mitigation

Smart contracts can be programmed to respond to specific security incidents in real time. For instance, they can trigger specific countermeasures, such as dynamically updating firewall rules when a potential threat is detected.

Case Studies of Smart Contract Applications in Cybersecurity

1. Decentralized Access Control: A case study of a blockchain-based access control system for a corporate network. Smart contracts manage access rights, automatically updating them based on employee roles and profiles.
2. Automated Patch Management: An example of how smart contracts have been used to manage and distribute security patches in an enterprise network. The smart contract ensures that only verified patches are deployed and that they are applied across the network promptly.
3. Incident Response in Financial Transactions: An instance where smart contracts have been used in financial networks to detect and respond to suspicious transactions automatically. The smart contract can temporarily freeze transactions or accounts that exhibit signs of fraudulent activity pending further investigation.

Integrating blockchain into existing network infrastructures for enhanced cybersecurity presents several technical and scalability challenges and considerations regarding latency and resource overheads. While the benefits of blockchain in terms of security and integrity are clear, its implementation in real-world scenarios requires careful planning and consideration of potential drawbacks.

One of the primary challenges lies in the technical complexities involved in blockchain integration. Existing network infrastructures and security protocols are often not designed to accommodate blockchain technology, which requires a fundamental shift in data management and security approaches. This shift involves technological changes and a rethinking of organizational processes and policies. While offering security benefits, blockchain's decentralized nature also means a departure from traditional centralized control mechanisms, which can be a significant hurdle for many organizations.

Scalability is another critical concern. Blockchain networks, particularly those employing proof of work (PoW) consensus mechanisms, can face transaction processing capacity and speed limitations. This limitation becomes especially pronounced in large-scale deployments or in applications requiring real-time processing. The scalability challenge is not just about handling large volumes of transactions but also about ensuring that the network can grow and adapt without compromising performance or security.

Latency and resource overheads are closely linked to scalability issues. Blockchain networks, due to their distributed ledger technology, can introduce latency in transaction processing, which might not be acceptable in scenarios requiring instant response, such as real-time threat detection and mitigation in cybersecurity. Additionally, the computational and storage resources required to maintain a blockchain network are significant. This resource overhead can be a concern for organizations, especially those with limited IT infrastructure and budgets.

Despite these challenges, the future prospects for blockchain in cybersecurity are promising, with several emerging trends and ongoing developments. One such trend is the increasing use of more energy-efficient consensus algorithms, such as proof of stake (PoS), which address some of the scalability and resource usage issues associated with PoW systems. There is also a growing interest in private or permissioned blockchains, which offer a balance between the decentralized nature of public blockchains and the control and efficiency of traditional centralized systems.

Ongoing research in blockchain technology is exploring ways to enhance its integration into cybersecurity solutions. This includes developing more scalable blockchain architectures, improving interoperability between different blockchain platforms, and creating frameworks for seamless integration with existing IT infrastructure. Researchers are also investigating the potential of blockchain in emerging areas such as quantum-resistant cryptography and secure multi-party computation, which could further strengthen cybersecurity measures.

4.7. Cloud-based Security Solutions

Advantages of Cloud-based Security Systems

1. Scalability and Flexibility: One of the most significant advantages of cloud-based security is its scalability. Organizations can easily adjust their security needs based on the current demand without the need for significant infrastructure changes. This scalability ensures that security measures can grow alongside the business, providing protection regardless of the size of the network or the volume of data.

2. Cost-Effectiveness: Cloud-based solutions often reduce the overall cost of security infrastructure. Traditional security systems require significant capital investment in hardware and software, along with ongoing maintenance costs. In contrast, cloud security typically operates on a subscription model, which can be more affordable and predictable in terms of budgeting.

3. Access to Advanced Security Tools: Cloud providers often offer access to state-of-the-art security tools and technologies. These tools include advanced threat detection systems, encryption services, and identity management solutions. Small and medium-sized businesses, in particular,

benefit from access to high-level security resources that would otherwise be cost-prohibitive.

4. Regular Updates and Maintenance: Cloud security providers handle the maintenance and updating of security systems. This service ensures that defenses are always up-to-date with the latest security patches and upgrades, a critical aspect of defending against new and evolving cyber threats.

5. Centralized Security Management: With cloud-based security, organizations can manage their security protocols from a centralized platform. This centralization makes it easier to monitor network activities, enforce policies, and respond to incidents quickly and effectively.

6. Reduced Downtime and Improved Recovery: Cloud services often include robust disaster recovery and redundancy systems. This setup ensures minimal downtime in the event of a cyber-attack and aids in faster recovery, thereby minimizing the impact on business operations.

How the Cloud Supports Autonomous Security

1. Data Aggregation and Analysis: Cloud platforms are inherently well-suited for aggregating vast amounts of data from various sources. This capability is crucial for AI-driven autonomous security systems, which rely on large datasets to train and refine their algorithms for threat detection and response.
2. Real-time Threat Intelligence: Cloud services can provide real-time threat intelligence by continuously analyzing data patterns across a wide network of users. This collective

intelligence helps in identifying and responding to new threats more quickly than individual, isolated security systems.

3. Automated Security Updates and Patch Management: Cloud-based security systems can automate the process of updating and patching, ensuring that all parts of the network are protected against known vulnerabilities without manual intervention.
4. Integration of AI and Machine Learning: The cloud provides the necessary computational power and storage capacity to effectively run AI and machine learning algorithms. These technologies enable the autonomous identification of suspicious activities, prediction of potential threats, and initiation of appropriate responses without human input.
5. Enhanced Collaboration and Sharing of Best Practices: Cloud platforms facilitate improved collaboration between various stakeholders in cybersecurity. Sharing insights, best practices, and threat intelligence among cloud users can lead to more robust and collectively smarter security systems.
6. Global Accessibility and Monitoring: Being hosted on the cloud, these security solutions offer the advantage of global accessibility. Security teams can monitor and manage network security from anywhere, at any time, which is crucial for organizations operating across multiple locations or time zones.

4.8. Edge Computing and IoT Security

Edge computing represents a significant shift in data processing, moving it closer to the data source. This approach contrasts with traditional centralized models where data is sent to distant data centers for processing. In the context of network security, edge computing implies that each device or local server possesses the capability to process and analyze data independently. This decentralization of data processing plays a critical role in enhancing the security of networks, especially in environments densely populated with IoT devices.

The concept of edge computing is particularly relevant in scenarios where real-time processing and decision-making are essential. For instance, in a security context, if an IoT device detects a potential security threat, it can immediately process this information and take appropriate action rather than waiting for a central server to respond. This shift not only improves efficiency but also enhances the ability to mitigate risks promptly.

> Enhancing Security with Edge Computing:

- Reduced Latency:

In a cybersecurity context, latency is more than just a delay; it can be the difference between stopping a cyber-attack in its tracks or allowing it to cause significant damage. Edge computing minimizes this latency by processing data where it's generated. This immediacy is crucial for real-time threat detection and response, allowing for swift identification and mitigation of potential threats.

For example, in a network with edge computing capabilities, an intrusion detection system located at the network's edge can instantly analyze traffic patterns and flag anomalies, leading to faster response times compared to a centralized system.

⟐ Data Sovereignty and Privacy:

With edge computing, data can be processed locally, reducing the need to send sensitive information across potentially insecure networks. This approach significantly minimizes the risk of data interception and leakage.

It also addresses data sovereignty concerns, as data does not leave its origin country or region, which is increasingly important given the strict data protection laws in various jurisdictions.

Moreover, local processing of data ensures compliance with privacy regulations, as sensitive information is less likely to be exposed to third-party services or transit networks.

⟐ Distributed Security Protocols:

Edge computing facilitates the implementation of security measures directly at the device level. This decentralized approach allows for more tailored and effective security protocols, catering to the specific needs and vulnerabilities of each device.

By embedding security protocols into edge devices, networks can prevent single points of failure. If one device is compromised, the breach does not necessarily propagate through the entire network.

This distributed nature of edge computing also aids in resilience. In case of an attack on central systems, edge devices can continue to operate independently, maintaining critical functions and security measures.

› Securing IoT Devices

Vulnerabilities in IoT:

Expanding Attack Surfaces: IoT devices, by their sheer numbers and connectivity, significantly broaden the attack surface in any network. These devices often come equipped with minimal security features, making them susceptible to cyberattacks. Common vulnerabilities include weak passwords, unsecured network services, and insecure interfaces. Diverse and Unstandardized Nature: The IoT ecosystem is characterized by a wide variety of devices, ranging from smart home appliances to industrial sensors, each with its own set of configurations, operating systems, and security capabilities. This diversity makes it challenging to apply uniform security measures, leaving gaps that can be exploited by cyber attackers.

Strategies for Securing IoT:

1. Device-Level Security: The first line of defense in securing IoT devices involves embedding robust security protocols directly into them. This includes secure boot processes to ensure the device boots with verified and untampered software, strong authentication mechanisms to prevent unauthorized access, and encryption of data both at rest and in transit to protect sensitive information.
2. Regular Software Updates and Patch Management: Manufacturers must provide regular firmware updates to address newly discovered vulnerabilities. Effective patch management strategies are crucial to ensure these updates are deployed promptly across all devices, minimizing the window of opportunity for attackers.
3. Network Segmentation: Dividing the network into smaller segments, with IoT devices isolated in their dedicated segments, can significantly reduce the risk of a network-wide breach. This strategy limits the access of IoT devices to only essential resources and services, containing potential breaches within a segment.
4. Behavioral Analysis and Anomaly Detection: Leveraging AI and machine learning, network security systems can continuously monitor the behavior of IoT devices for any anomalies that could indicate a security threat, such as unusual data traffic or uncharacteristic operations. These systems can quickly identify and isolate compromised devices, mitigating potential damage.
5. Edge Analytics for Real-Time Security: Utilizing edge computing for real-time data analysis enables immediate detection and response to security incidents at the device level. By processing data locally, edge devices can rapidly identify and respond to threats without the latency involved in sending data to a central server for analysis.

Challenges in IoT Security:

1. Resource Constraints: IoT devices often have limited processing power and memory, which can constrain the implementation of advanced security measures. This limitation necessitates the development of lightweight, efficient security protocols that can operate effectively within these constraints.

2. Scale of Deployment: The massive scale of IoT device deployment presents logistical challenges in maintaining consistent and up-to-date security across all devices. This issue is compounded by the long lifespan of many IoT devices, which may outlive the support period provided by the manufacturer.

3. Interoperability: IoT devices often need to communicate and work together, sometimes across different manufacturers and ecosystems. This interoperability, while beneficial for functionality, introduces additional security challenges, as vulnerabilities in one device or system can potentially be exploited to compromise connected devices.

4.9. Adaptive Security Architecture

Adaptive Security Architecture (ASA) is a dynamic approach to cybersecurity designed to continuously adjust and evolve in response to a changing threat landscape. Unlike traditional security measures, which often rely on predefined rules and static defenses, ASA is characterized by its agility and responsiveness. It leverages advanced technologies like AI, machine learning, and real-time data analytics to assess risks and adapt its defenses.

The core idea behind ASA is to anticipate, prevent, detect, and respond to threats in a continuous cycle rather than relying on periodic updates or manual interventions. This approach recognizes that cyber threats are not static and that security systems must be equally dynamic to be effective.

Benefits of Adaptive Security Architecture

Adaptive Security Architecture offers a comprehensive approach to cybersecurity, characterized by its dynamic and proactive nature. One of the key advantages of this approach is its anticipatory threat detection capability. By leveraging advanced analytics and threat intelligence, ASA is adept at foreseeing and identifying potential threats before they escalate into actual attacks.

Another significant benefit is the immediate, adaptive response to identified threats. This responsiveness allows ASA systems to swiftly adapt and mitigate risks as they arise, dramatically reducing the potential for damage. The architecture's ability to reconfigure its defenses in real time is a testament to its flexibility and responsiveness to the evolving threat landscape.

Continuous learning and enhancement are at the heart of ASA. By constantly evolving based on data from past incidents and global cybersecurity trends, these systems refine their threat detection and response mechanisms, staying several steps ahead of cybercriminals.

A key advantage of ASA is the minimized necessity for human oversight. By automating critical security responses, the system reduces the reliance on constant human supervision. This automation allows cybersecurity personnel to focus on strategic initiatives rather than routine monitoring, enhancing overall security efficiency.

ASA's adaptability to evolving IT landscapes is another vital benefit. Its scalable nature ensures robust security across various IT infrastructures, including cloud-based, on-premises, and hybrid environments. This flexibility is crucial for modern organizations that operate across diverse technological platforms.

Finally, streamlined compliance and risk management are inherent in ASA's design. Its capability to quickly adapt to new regulations and compliance standards ensures that organizations remain compliant with evolving legal and industry requirements, thus mitigating legal and operational risks.

Case Studies of Adaptive Security in Action

1. Financial Sector Implementation:

A major bank deployed an ASA system to protect against sophisticated phishing attacks. The system used AI to analyze email patterns and user behavior, identifying and neutralizing phishing attempts before they reach end-users. This proactive approach significantly reduced financial fraud incidents.

2. Healthcare Data Protection:

A healthcare provider implemented ASA to secure patient data. The system utilized machine learning to monitor network traffic and detect anomalies indicative of data breaches or unauthorized access. As a result, the provider successfully thwarted multiple data exfiltration attempts, safeguarding sensitive patient information.

3. Retail Industry's Response to POS Attacks:

A global retail chain adopted ASA to protect against Point-of-Sale (POS) system breaches. The adaptive security system dynamically adjusted its security protocols based on real-time transaction data, effectively identifying and isolating suspicious activities, thereby preventing large-scale data theft.

4. Government Infrastructure Defense:

A government agency implemented ASA to defend critical infrastructure. The system used advanced analytics to monitor and adapt to threats against physical and digital assets. By integrating IoT device security, the agency enhanced its overall resilience against both cyber and physical threats.

CHAPTER 5: THREAT DETECTION AND RESPONSE

In the ever-evolving landscape of cybersecurity, the advent of Artificial Intelligence (AI) has revolutionized how threats are detected and responded to. Traditionally, cybersecurity hinged on signature-based and rule-based methods that primarily focused on known threats. These methods, while effective against familiar dangers, were often inadequate against novel or rapidly mutating cyber threats. AI-driven threat detection marks a significant shift towards a more proactive and dynamic approach.

AI in cybersecurity utilizes machine learning algorithms to analyze patterns and anomalies that could indicate a threat. This shift from a reactive to a predictive approach empowers organizations to anticipate and mitigate threats before they cause harm.

5.1. Understanding AI in Threat Detection

The Fundamentals of AI in Cybersecurity

At the core of AI-driven threat detection is the ability of AI systems to analyze, learn, and make decisions based on vast amounts of data. Unlike traditional security systems that follow predefined rules, AI systems continually evolve their understanding of what constitutes normal and abnormal behavior within a network. This is achieved through the application of various machine-learning techniques.

Machine Learning Techniques in Cybersecurity

1. Supervised Learning: This is the most commonly used technique in AI threat detection. Here, the AI model is trained on a labeled dataset, where each piece of data is tagged as either 'normal' or 'threat.' The model learns to distinguish between these two categories, enabling it to identify known threats accurately. This approach is particularly effective against malware, ransomware, and phishing attacks.
2. Unsupervised Learning: In contrast to supervised learning, unsupervised learning involves training the model on data that is not labeled. The AI system learns to identify patterns and anomalies on its own. This method is crucial for detecting new or evolving threats that have not been seen before. It can recognize suspicious activities based on deviations from established patterns, making it a vital tool for identifying zero-day exploits and advanced persistent threats (APTs).
3. Semi-Supervised Learning: This technique combines elements of both supervised and unsupervised learning. It is particularly useful when there is a limited amount of labeled data available. The system uses the labeled data to learn certain features and then applies this understanding to a larger, unlabeled dataset.
4. Reinforcement Learning: A relatively new approach in cybersecurity, reinforcement learning involves training the model through a system of rewards and penalties. The AI learns to make decisions that maximize the reward outcome. This technique is being explored for developing adaptive threat response systems where the AI must make complex decisions in dynamic environments.

Deep Learning in Threat Detection

Deep learning, a subset of machine learning, involves neural networks with multiple layers that enable the processing of vast amounts of data with intricate structures. In threat detection, deep learning is particularly useful for identifying complex patterns that simpler machine learning models might miss. For example, deep learning algorithms are adept at analyzing network traffic in real-time to detect subtle signs of intrusion or exfiltration.

Challenges in AI Model Training

Training AI models for cybersecurity poses its own set of challenges. One significant issue is the need for extensive and relevant training data. The quality and diversity of this data directly impact the effectiveness of the AI system. There is also the risk of 'model drift,' where the model's accuracy degrades over time as threats evolve, necessitating regular updates and retraining.

Integrating AI into Existing Cybersecurity Frameworks

Integrating AI into existing cybersecurity infrastructures requires careful planning. AI systems need to work in harmony with existing security protocols and tools. This integration often involves a phased approach, starting with AI as a supplementary tool to existing security measures and gradually increasing its role as the system's reliability is proven.

5.2 Automated Response Mechanisms

The Mechanism of Automated Responses

When an AI system detects a potential threat, the response must be swift and precise. Automated response mechanisms are designed to act immediately upon detection, minimizing the window of opportunity for the threat to cause harm. These responses can range from simple notifications to security teams to complex autonomous actions.

One common automated response is the immediate isolation of affected systems or network segments. This action, often referred to as 'auto-quarantining,' helps contain the threat and prevent its spread across the network. In more advanced setups, AI systems can also initiate processes to patch vulnerabilities or update security protocols in real-time, further fortifying the network against similar attacks.

Integration with Incident Response Plans

Effective automated response mechanisms are not standalone solutions; they are integrated into a broader incident response plan. This integration ensures that automated actions align with the organization's overall security policies and strategies. For example, in critical infrastructure systems, automated responses might be more conservative to avoid unintended disruptions of essential services.

Adaptive Response Strategies

One of the most significant advantages of AI-driven systems is their ability to adapt and learn. Over time, these systems can analyze the outcomes of their responses, learning to distinguish between effective and ineffective actions. This adaptive capability allows for the refinement of response strategies, ensuring that they become more accurate and efficient.

Challenges in Automation

Despite the advantages, automated response systems face several challenges. One major challenge is the balance between speed and accuracy. Rapid responses are essential, but they must be tempered with the need to avoid false positives, which can disrupt normal operations or lead to unintended consequences.

Another challenge is the complexity of managing and updating these systems. As cyber threats evolve, so must the response mechanisms. This requires continuous monitoring, updating of AI models, and regular testing to ensure that responses remain effective against new and sophisticated threats.

Ethical and Legal Considerations

Automated responses, especially those that involve proactive measures like counterattacks or disabling systems, raise ethical and legal considerations. The decision-making process of an AI system in such scenarios must be transparent and aligned with legal and ethical standards. This alignment is crucial to maintain trust and ensure accountability in the use of AI in cybersecurity.

Case Studies

1. Case Study 1: Financial Institution Thwarts Phishing Attack

In one landmark instance, a major financial institution employed an AI-driven security system that showcased the power of machine learning in identifying and mitigating cyber threats. The institution faced a sophisticated phishing attack aimed at high-value accounts. Traditional security measures were bypassing these attacks due to their advanced obfuscation techniques.

The AI system, trained on vast datasets including previous phishing attempts, identified the attack by recognizing subtle patterns in the email traffic that deviated from the norm. Upon detection, the system automatically triggered protective measures, including alerting security personnel, quarantining affected emails, and blocking phishing sources. This prompt response averted potential financial losses and data breaches.

1. Case Study 2: Healthcare Provider Prevents Ransomware Disaster

A healthcare provider implemented an AI-based cybersecurity system as part of its network security upgrade. Shortly after deployment, the system detected unusual activity in the network indicative of a ransomware attack in its early stages. By analyzing the encryption patterns and comparing them with known ransomware signatures, the AI system identified the threat before it could encrypt critical patient data.

The AI system's response was swift and decisive. It isolated the infected segments of the network, preventing the ransomware from spreading further. Simultaneously, it notified the cybersecurity team, who then implemented additional countermeasures. This early detection and response were crucial in maintaining the integrity of the healthcare provider's data and ensuring continuous patient care.

1. Case Study 3: Retail Giant Combats Point-of-Sale Breach

A global retail company faced a point-of-sale (POS) system breach, where attackers attempted to siphon credit card information from thousands of transactions. The company's AI-driven security system, equipped with advanced anomaly detection capabilities, identified irregularities in data transmission from POS terminals.

Utilizing real-time analysis, the AI system was able to differentiate between normal transaction patterns and anomalous data exfiltration attempts. Upon detection, the system immediately alerted the security team and initiated protocols to block the unauthorized data transmissions. This intervention not only prevented a massive data breach but also enabled the company to track and strengthen vulnerabilities in its POS systems.

1. Case Study 4: Utility Company Mitigates DDoS Attack

A large utility company faced a Distributed Denial of Service (DDoS) attack aimed at disrupting its operations. Their AI-based cybersecurity system, designed to monitor network traffic, detected the attack almost immediately. The system recognized the abnormal surge in traffic as a potential DDoS attack by comparing it to historical traffic data.

The AI system's automated response mechanisms kicked in, rerouting traffic and filtering out malicious data packets. Additionally, its deployed countermeasures to absorb and dissipate the attack's impact. This proactive response ensured that the utility company's operations remained uninterrupted, showcasing the effectiveness of AI in handling large-scale cyber threats.

Challenges and Considerations in AI-Driven Systems

> The Complexity of False Positives and Negatives

One of the most significant challenges in AI-driven systems is the management of false positives and negatives. False positives, where benign activities are incorrectly flagged as threats, can lead to unnecessary disruptions and resource wastage. Conversely, false negatives, where actual threats go undetected, pose a grave security risk. Balancing the sensitivity of AI models to minimize both is a complex task requiring continuous refinement and adjustment.

> Evolving Cyber Threat Landscape

The cyber threat landscape is continuously evolving, with attackers constantly developing new methods to bypass security systems. This fluidity presents a significant challenge for AI-driven systems, which need to be perpetually trained with the latest threat data. The risk here is that an AI system trained on outdated information becomes less effective, potentially leaving systems vulnerable to new types of attacks.

> Ethical and Privacy Concerns

As AI systems in cybersecurity often process large amounts of data, including potentially sensitive personal information, privacy concerns are paramount. Ethical considerations also emerge in decisions made by AI systems, particularly in automated responses. Ensuring transparency and accountability in AI decisions is crucial to maintaining trust and compliance with regulatory standards.

> Dependency and Over-Reliance

There's a risk of over-reliance on AI systems, leading to a potential erosion of human expertise in cybersecurity. While AI enhances efficiency and effectiveness, it should complement, not replace, human oversight. This balance is crucial to ensure that AI systems are monitored and managed by skilled professionals who can intervene when necessary.

The Future of Threat Detection and Response

> Integration of Emerging Technologies

The future of threat detection and response is likely to be marked by the integration of emerging technologies. Developments in areas such as deep learning, quantum computing, and blockchain could offer new ways to enhance AI-driven security systems. For example, quantum computing might enable the processing of massive datasets at unprecedented speeds, allowing for more sophisticated and rapid threat detection.

> Adaptive and Self-Learning Systems

The next generation of AI in cybersecurity will likely focus on adaptive and self-learning systems capable of evolving in response to changing threat patterns. These systems would not only detect and respond to threats but also learn from each interaction, continuously improving their effectiveness.

> Proactive and Predictive Security Models

Shifting from a reactive to a proactive stance, future AI systems are expected to predict and neutralize threats before they materialize. By analyzing trends and patterns, these systems could foresee potential vulnerabilities and recommend preemptive measures, thereby staying a step ahead of attackers.

› Human-AI Collaboration

Emphasizing the importance of human-AI collaboration, future models of threat detection and response will likely foster a symbiotic relationship between AI systems and cybersecurity professionals. This collaboration ensures that the intuitive and creative problem-solving abilities of humans complement the analytical and processing powers of AI.

› Global Collaboration and Standardization

As cyber threats become more global and sophisticated, there will be a growing need for international collaboration and standardization in AI-driven security solutions. This global approach would facilitate the sharing of threat intelligence and best practices, enhancing the collective defense against cyber threats.

CHAPTER 6: CHALLENGES AND LIMITATIONS

6.1. Introduction to the Real-World Complexities

The Dual Nature of AI in Cybersecurity

The integration of Artificial Intelligence (AI) in cybersecurity is a groundbreaking advancement, offering unprecedented capabilities in threat detection and response. However, this innovation comes with its own set of complexities. AI's transformative potential in cybersecurity is a double-edged sword; it's a powerful tool in combating cyber threats but also presents new challenges that must be carefully navigated.

Understanding the Cybersecurity Landscape

The field of cybersecurity is inherently dynamic and complex. Cyber threats evolve rapidly, as do the technologies designed to combat them. In this ever-changing landscape, AI systems must be agile and adaptive. However, the implementation of AI in such a volatile environment is fraught with challenges. These range from technical limitations to ethical considerations, each adding layers of complexity to the cybersecurity paradigm.

AI's Potential and Limitations

AI in cybersecurity promises enhanced efficiency, speed, and accuracy in threat detection and response. By leveraging vast datasets and sophisticated algorithms, AI systems can identify patterns and anomalies that might elude human analysts. Yet, this potential is not without limitations. AI systems are only as good as the data they analyze and the algorithms they employ. Any shortfall in these areas can significantly diminish their effectiveness.

Navigating the Complexity

Implementing AI in cybersecurity requires a careful balance. On one hand, there's a need to harness AI's full potential to stay ahead of sophisticated cyber threats. On the other, there's a pressing need to address the inherent limitations and challenges of AI technologies. This includes managing issues related to data quality, algorithmic biases, computational demands, and ethical considerations.

The Human Element

While AI brings automation and efficiency, the human element remains indispensable. AI systems need continuous oversight, fine-tuning, and ethical guidance from cybersecurity professionals. This human-AI collaboration is crucial in addressing the real-world complexities of AI in cybersecurity.

6.2: Technical Limitations of Current AI Systems

› Data Dependency

In the dynamic landscape of cybersecurity, where threats evolve rapidly, AI systems play a vital role in identifying and mitigating risks. However, the effectiveness of these AI systems is profoundly influenced by the quality and quantity of data they rely on.

- The Need for Quality Data

AI systems thrive on data; they are data-hungry engines that rely on vast datasets to learn and make informed decisions. The axiom "garbage in, garbage out" holds true in the cybersecurity context. To make accurate predictions and detect anomalies, AI systems require high-quality data that reflects the current threat landscape.

- Challenges in Data Acquisition

Obtaining this high-quality data in the cybersecurity domain is not a straightforward task. Data sources are often dispersed, heterogeneous, and may not be readily accessible. Furthermore, the sensitive nature of cybersecurity data, including network traffic logs and incident reports, adds a layer of complexity to data acquisition.

- Risk of Outdated or Biased Data

Another challenge stems from the temporality and bias in cybersecurity data. Historical data, while informative, may not reflect emerging threats, rendering AI models less effective in dealing with novel attack vectors. Additionally, biases present in historical data can propagate into AI models, potentially leading to unfair or discriminatory outcomes.

› Algorithmic Limitations

While AI algorithms have shown remarkable capabilities in various domains, they are not infallible, and their limitations become particularly evident in the intricate world of cybersecurity.

- Accuracy Concerns

Cybersecurity demands a high degree of precision. False positives can lead to alert fatigue, where security professionals are overwhelmed with non-critical notifications, potentially missing real threats. Conversely, false negatives can allow malicious activities to go undetected. Achieving the delicate balance between true positives and true negatives is challenging.

- Adapting to Novel Threats

The cybersecurity landscape is in a perpetual state of evolution, with cybercriminals constantly devising new tactics and attack vectors. Current AI systems, primarily trained on historical data, may struggle to adapt to these novel threats. They can be blindsided by innovative attack methods that have not been encountered before.

- Generalization vs. Specialization

AI models must strike a balance between generalization and specialization. A highly specialized model may excel in one aspect of cybersecurity but falter when faced with a different kind of threat. Conversely, overly generalized models may miss subtle nuances that are critical in identifying sophisticated attacks.

› Computational Requirements

The computational demands of AI systems in cybersecurity are substantial, and this poses practical challenges for organizations, especially smaller ones.

- Resource-Intensive Nature of AI

AI, particularly deep learning algorithms, is resource-intensive. Training and running complex AI models require significant computational power, including specialized hardware like GPUs. The computational hunger of AI can strain an organization's IT infrastructure.

- The barrier to Entry for Smaller Organizations

For smaller organizations with limited resources, the barrier to entry into AI-driven cybersecurity can be high. The costs associated with acquiring and maintaining the necessary computational infrastructure can be prohibitive, potentially leaving them at a disadvantage in defending against cyber threats.

- Energy and Cost Implications

Beyond the immediate costs, there are broader implications related to energy consumption and operational expenses. Running resource-intensive AI models can have environmental and financial consequences, which organizations must consider.

6.3. Security Vulnerabilities of AI Systems

Adversarial Attacks: Adversarial attacks refer to a technique where attackers intentionally manipulate inputs to AI systems to deceive them or cause misclassifications. In the context of cybersecurity, this can have severe consequences.

Here's how it works:

1. Gradient-based Attacks: Attackers use techniques to compute the gradient of the AI model's loss function with respect to the input data. By making small, imperceptible changes to input data (e.g., an image or a piece of code), they can maximize the model's prediction error.
2. Manipulating Security Features: Attackers can target security systems that use AI, such as intrusion detection systems. By crafting malicious inputs, they can evade detection or trigger false alarms. For example, in network traffic analysis, an attacker might manipulate packets to bypass detection mechanisms.
3. Causative Attacks: These attacks go beyond evasion and aim to cause a specific action or response from the AI system. For instance, attackers might manipulate an autonomous security

system to block legitimate user access.

4. Transferability: Adversarial attacks are often transferable, meaning an attack that works against one AI model can also work against similar models, making it a scalable threat.

The impact of adversarial attacks on cybersecurity can lead to false negatives, where genuine threats are missed, or false positives, where benign inputs are flagged as malicious. To counter these threats, cybersecurity professionals need to develop robust AI models that are resilient to adversarial manipulation and implement continuous monitoring to detect and respond to such attacks.

6.4. Ethical and Privacy Concerns

› **Privacy Issues:** AI systems often require access to extensive datasets for training and continuous learning. While this data is pivotal in enhancing cybersecurity, it raises a plethora of privacy concerns that must not be overlooked:

1. Data Collection and Storage: AI systems may collect and store vast amounts of data, including personally identifiable information (PII). Unauthorized access or data breaches can lead to the exposure of sensitive information.
2. Data Processing: The processing of data by AI systems can uncover hidden patterns and insights. While invaluable for cybersecurity, it also raises concerns about how this information is used and whether it is adequately protected.
3. Data Retention: Decisions regarding how long data is retained and for what purposes can significantly impact privacy. Retaining data for extended periods increases the risk of exposure in case of a breach.
4. Consent and Transparency: Individuals may not be aware of how their data is used by AI systems, and obtaining informed consent for data usage can be a complex undertaking.

› Bias and Fairness

Bias and Fairness: Ethical considerations become paramount when dealing with AI systems in cybersecurity, as they are trained on historical data that may contain inherent biases. These biases can manifest in various ways:

I. Discriminatory Outcomes: Biased AI systems may unfairly target certain groups or individuals, leading to discrimination or inequitable treatment in cybersecurity processes.
II. Inaccurate Threat Detection: Bias in training data can result in the misclassification of threats, either by overemphasizing some types of threats or by neglecting others.
III. Loss of Trust: Fairness issues can erode trust in AI-driven security systems, both within organizations and among users and customers, potentially undermining the effectiveness of these systems.

Addressing privacy and bias concerns in AI cybersecurity requires a multifaceted approach. It involves careful data selection, preprocessing, and ongoing monitoring to ensure that privacy is respected and biases are minimized. Ethical considerations must be an integral part of the development and deployment of AI systems to prevent discriminatory outcomes, ensure equitable protection, and uphold user trust.

6.5. Integration Challenges

- **Compatibility with Existing Systems**

1. Diverse Ecosystems: The challenge of integrating AI solutions into existing security infrastructure often arises from the diversity of technologies in use. Organizations may have invested in various security tools, each from different vendors, to address specific aspects of cybersecurity. Ensuring compatibility between these tools and new AI-driven solutions can be complex. It may require significant effort to make them work together seamlessly.
2. Data Sharing: AI systems thrive on data, especially in cybersecurity. However, integrating AI into legacy systems may require establishing data-sharing protocols and APIs. This can be a time-consuming process and can introduce potential security risks if not implemented carefully. Organizations need to strike a balance between sharing enough data for AI to be effective and protecting sensitive information.
3. Skill Gaps: Successful integration of AI solutions often depends on the availability of skilled personnel. Organizations may need to invest in training or hiring experts who understand both AI and cybersecurity. These experts can bridge the gap between existing security teams and the new

AI-driven technologies, ensuring a smooth integration process.

4. Legacy Constraints: Some legacy systems may have limitations in terms of their compatibility with modern AI technologies. They may lack the necessary interfaces or have outdated hardware that cannot support AI applications. Decisions may need to be made about whether to upgrade or replace certain legacy components to facilitate integration.
5. Phased Approach: Organizations may opt for a phased approach to integration. This involves gradually introducing AI capabilities into the existing ecosystem, allowing for testing and adjustment along the way. It can help minimize disruptions and identify compatibility issues early.

- **User Trust and Reliance**

1. Skepticism: Users, including security professionals, may express skepticism about the capabilities of AI in cybersecurity. They may question whether AI can truly understand the nuances of evolving threats and adapt to them effectively. This skepticism can result in resistance to fully embracing AI-driven solutions.
2. Over-Reliance: On the flip side, there's a risk of over-reliance on AI. Some users may develop blind trust in automated systems, assuming that AI can handle all security tasks without human intervention. This over-reliance can be dangerous as it may lead to neglect of essential security practices and the human expertise needed to address unique situations.
3. Education and Communication: Building trust while avoiding over-reliance is a delicate balance. Organizations must invest in educating their staff about the capabilities and

limitations of AI systems. Clear communication about the role of AI in cybersecurity and the continued importance of human oversight is essential.

4. Human-AI Collaboration: Emphasizing the concept of human-AI collaboration can help address trust issues. AI can excel in tasks that involve processing vast amounts of data quickly, while humans excel in critical thinking and decision-making. Highlighting the synergy between human expertise and AI capabilities can foster a more balanced approach.
5. Transparency: Transparency in AI decision-making processes is crucial for user trust. Users need to understand how AI arrives at its conclusions and recommendations. AI systems should be designed to provide explanations for their actions, helping users make informed decisions.

6.6. Regulatory and Compliance Issues

- **Evolving Regulations**

The landscape of cybersecurity regulations is constantly evolving to keep pace with technological advancements. When it comes to AI in cybersecurity, these regulatory changes bring both opportunities and challenges:

1. Data Privacy Regulations: Evolving data privacy regulations, such as the General Data Protection Regulation (GDPR) in Europe and the California Consumer Privacy Act (CCPA), impose strict requirements on how organizations collect, store, and process personal data. AI systems must comply with these regulations, which often require explicit user consent and transparent data-handling practices.

2. Algorithmic Transparency: Some regulations, particularly in the European Union, emphasize the need for transparency in AI decision-making processes. This means that organizations deploying AI in cybersecurity must ensure that their AI algorithms are explainable and understandable to users and regulators. Achieving this transparency can be challenging, especially when dealing with complex machine learning models.

3. Cross-Border Data Flow: In today's globalized world, data often flows across borders. Different regions have their own data protection laws, and these regulations can conflict. Organizations operating internationally must navigate the complex landscape of international data transfer regulations to ensure that their AI-driven security solutions comply with the laws of each jurisdiction.

- **Compliance Complexity**

Ensuring compliance with a myriad of regulations and standards is a complex undertaking, and AI introduces additional layers of complexity:

1. Customization for Different Regions: AI solutions may need to be customized to meet the specific compliance requirements of different regions or sectors. For example, what is considered compliant in one jurisdiction may not be in another. Organizations must navigate these variations while maintaining a unified security strategy.

2. Documentation and Auditing: Regulatory compliance often requires organizations to maintain detailed documentation of AI processes and conduct regular audits. This documentation includes data handling practices, algorithmic decision-making procedures, and security protocols. Auditing AI systems can be resource-intensive and requires expertise in both AI and compliance.

3. Liability Considerations: Determining liability in the event of a security breach involving AI systems can be complex. Regulations may evolve to address issues of responsibility and accountability in cases where AI decisions

lead to security incidents. Organizations must stay updated on these regulatory changes and adapt their policies accordingly.

4. Risk Assessment: Compliance requires organizations to conduct risk assessments to identify potential vulnerabilities and mitigate them. This process must include an evaluation of the AI-driven security measures in place and their effectiveness in addressing regulatory requirements.

6.7. The Future Landscape of AI Challenges

- **Evolving Threats**

The dynamic nature of cybersecurity threats presents an ongoing challenge for AI systems:

1. Zero-Day Attacks: Threat actors are continually devising new, previously unknown attack methods known as zero-day attacks. These attacks target vulnerabilities that have not yet been identified or patched. AI systems must be capable of detecting and responding to zero-day attacks without prior knowledge or signatures. This requires advanced anomaly detection and behavioral analysis.

2. AI-Powered Attacks: As AI technology becomes more accessible, cybercriminals may harness its capabilities to create more sophisticated and evasive attacks. AI-driven attacks can adapt in real time, making them particularly challenging to counter. AI systems must not only defend against these attacks but also leverage AI for threat detection and prevention.

3. Adaptive Adversaries: Attackers are increasingly adaptive and responsive to defensive measures. AI systems must

anticipate the adaptability of adversaries and proactively evolve their defense strategies. This involves continuous learning and adaptation to stay one step ahead of cybercriminals.

4. Regulatory Responses: Governments and regulatory bodies worldwide are recognizing the importance of cybersecurity. As cyber threats evolve, regulations and compliance requirements are likely to become more stringent. Organizations deploying AI in cybersecurity must navigate these evolving regulatory landscapes to ensure compliance while maintaining effective security measures.

- **Sustainability Concerns**

The environmental impact of AI, especially deep learning models, is an emerging concern:

1. Energy Consumption: Training and running AI models, especially large-scale deep learning models, can be extremely energy-intensive. Data centers and high-performance computing clusters consume vast amounts of electricity, contributing to carbon emissions. Organizations are under pressure to explore energy-efficient AI training methods and hardware.

2. Hardware Footprint: The hardware infrastructure required to support AI workloads, including GPUs and specialized accelerators, can have a substantial physical footprint. The manufacturing, deployment, and eventual disposal of these components can contribute to e-waste. Sustainable AI initiatives aim to minimize hardware waste and promote responsible recycling practices.

3. Green AI Initiatives: In response to sustainability concerns, researchers and organizations are actively developing "green AI" solutions. These initiatives focus on reducing the energy consumption of AI models and optimizing their environmental impact. Techniques like model quantization, pruning, and efficient hardware design play a role in creating more eco-friendly AI systems.

Addressing these evolving challenges in the future landscape of AI in cybersecurity will require a proactive and adaptive approach. Organizations and researchers must collaborate to develop AI systems that can effectively counter emerging threats while minimizing their environmental footprint.

CHAPTER 7: FUTURE TRENDS AND PREDICTIONS

Emerging Trends in AI and Network Security

As we delve deeper into the nuances of AI in network security, it's essential to understand the emerging trends shaping this field. The rapid advancement of AI technologies and the evolving landscape of cyber threats are driving significant changes in how we approach network security. Here's a comprehensive exploration of these trends:

1. Enhanced Machine Learning and Deep Learning Techniques: The application of machine learning and deep learning in network security is rapidly advancing. These technologies are becoming more sophisticated in identifying patterns and anomalies that indicate potential security threats. For instance, deep learning can analyze vast amounts of network data to identify subtle patterns indicative of advanced persistent threats (APTs) and zero-day exploits, which are often undetectable by traditional security measures.
2. Predictive Analytics in Threat Detection: AI systems are increasingly being used for predictive analytics in cybersecurity. By analyzing historical data and current trends, AI can predict where vulnerabilities and threats might emerge in the future. This approach enables proactive security measures, allowing organizations to bolster defenses before an attack occurs.
3. Automated Threat Response and Mitigation: The trend towards automation in network security is significant. AI-driven systems can automatically respond to detected threats, reducing the time to respond and mitigating the impact of attacks. This automation extends to routine security tasks, freeing up human security experts to focus on more complex challenges.

4. AI in IoT Security: As the Internet of Things (IoT) grows, securing the plethora of connected devices becomes increasingly complex. AI is vital in monitoring and protecting these devices. It can analyze data from diverse sources, recognize patterns, and identify potential security breaches. AI-driven security is particularly crucial for IoT, where traditional security approaches may not be feasible due to hardware constraints.
5. Adaptive Security Architecture: Future network security solutions are expected to be more adaptive. AI systems will continually learn from network activity and adapt their security protocols dynamically. This adaptive approach means that security measures can evolve in response to changing network behaviors and emerging threats.
6. Integration of AI with Blockchain for Enhanced Security: Blockchain technology, known for its robustness and decentralized nature, is increasingly being integrated with AI for enhanced security solutions. This integration can offer improved data integrity, transparency, and traceability, making it harder for cyber attackers to manipulate or breach networks.
7. Behavioral Analytics for Insider Threat Detection: AI-driven behavioral analytics is becoming a key tool in detecting insider threats. By continuously monitoring user behaviors, AI can identify actions that deviate from the norm, potentially indicating malicious activities. This is particularly important as insider threats are often more difficult to detect than external attacks.
8. Quantum Computing and AI in Cybersecurity: The rise of quantum computing presents both challenges and opportunities. Quantum computers have the potential to break current encryption methods, necessitating new forms

of quantum-resistant cryptography. AI will play a crucial role in developing these new cryptographic techniques and in securing networks against quantum computing threats.

9. Ethical AI and Bias Mitigation in Security: As AI takes a central role in network security, the importance of ethical AI comes to the forefront. This includes ensuring that AI systems are transparent, explainable, and free from biases that could lead to unfair or ineffective security measures.
10. Collaboration and Information Sharing: AI systems are expected to enhance collaboration and information sharing among different security platforms and organizations. By leveraging AI, disparate systems can share threat intelligence in real-time, leading to a more coordinated and effective response to cyber threats.
11. Customizable AI Security Solutions: With the diversity in network architectures and the varying security needs of organizations, there is a growing trend towards customizable AI security solutions. These solutions can be tailored to specific network environments, offering more effective and efficient security.

Predictions for the Future of Autonomous Security

As we look towards the future, the landscape of autonomous security, particularly in the realm of network and cybersecurity, is poised for transformative changes. These predictions encapsulate the advancements, challenges, and evolving dynamics of the field.

1. Pervasive AI Integration: In the future, AI is expected to become a fundamental component in all aspects of network security. This integration will lead to systems that are not only reactive but also proactive in identifying and mitigating

threats. The AI will continually learn and adapt from each interaction, becoming more efficient in recognizing and responding to new types of cyberattacks.

2. Self-Learning and Self-Adapting Systems: Autonomous security systems will evolve to be self-learning and self-adapting. These systems will dynamically adjust their defense mechanisms based on evolving threats without human intervention. By analyzing patterns of attacks and system vulnerabilities, these intelligent systems can predict and prevent future attacks with greater accuracy.
3. Quantum Resilience: As quantum computing emerges, creating potential threats to traditional encryption methods, autonomous security systems will need to develop quantum-resilient encryption. AI will play a crucial role in creating and maintaining security protocols that can withstand the power of quantum computing.
4. Advanced Threat Detection and Response: Future autonomous security systems will utilize advanced threat detection algorithms that can identify even the most subtle and sophisticated attacks. They will be capable of instantaneously responding to these threats, mitigating damage, and learning from the incident to prevent similar attacks in the future.
5. Decentralized Security via Blockchain: The application of blockchain technology in network security will lead to more decentralized security frameworks. These frameworks will be less susceptible to single points of failure and can provide enhanced security for transactions and communications across networks.
6. Human-AI Collaborative Systems: While AI will play an increasingly significant role in autonomous security, human oversight will remain essential. Future systems will likely be

designed to enhance and complement human decision-making, ensuring that ethical considerations and nuanced judgments are not overlooked.

7. Enhanced Privacy Protections: With growing concerns about data privacy, future autonomous security systems will be designed with advanced privacy-preserving technologies. These technologies might include homomorphic encryption, allowing data to be processed in an encrypted form, and federated learning, where AI models are trained across multiple decentralized devices or servers without exchanging data samples.

1. Personalized Security Protocols: AI in autonomous security will enable the development of more personalized security protocols. This personalization will take into account individual user behavior, the specific needs of different devices, and the unique vulnerabilities of various networks to tailor security measures accordingly.
2. Regulatory and Ethical Frameworks: As AI becomes more prevalent in security, there will be a greater need for comprehensive regulatory and ethical frameworks. These frameworks will ensure that autonomous security systems operate within legal boundaries and ethical norms, particularly in terms of privacy, data usage, and decision-making processes.
3. Predictive Cybersecurity: Leveraging big data and advanced analytics, AI-driven security systems will move towards predictive cybersecurity. This approach will involve analyzing trends and predicting potential security breaches before they happen, allowing organizations to implement preemptive measures to avert these threats.
4. Cross-Domain AI Security Solutions: Future developments

may see AI security solutions that span across different domains, providing comprehensive protection that encompasses cloud services, IoT devices, enterprise networks, and personal devices. These solutions will offer a unified approach to security, capable of quickly sharing insights and defense strategies across various platforms.

5. AI in Cybersecurity Education and Training: The rise of AI in autonomous security will necessitate changes in cybersecurity education and training. Professionals in the field will need to understand AI methodologies and how to work alongside AI systems effectively.

CHAPTER 8: ETHICAL CONSIDERATIONS AND COMPLIANCE

8.1. Ethical Implications of AI in Cybersecurity

The ethical implications of AI in cybersecurity are both profound and multifaceted, reflecting a growing concern as AI systems increasingly become integral to protecting digital infrastructure. These implications span various dimensions, including societal impact, moral responsibility, and the inherent challenges posed by the technology itself.

1. **Implications of Bias and Discrimination:** One of the most significant ethical concerns is the potential for AI systems to propagate or even amplify biases. In cybersecurity, this issue manifests when AI-based systems are trained on datasets that are not representative of the full spectrum of cyber threats or user behaviors. This can lead to skewed security measures that unfairly target or overlook certain groups or behaviors. For instance, an AI system might flag activities as malicious based on biased data inputs, leading to wrongful accusations or unnecessary escalations.
2. **Privacy and Surveillance Concerns:** As AI systems in cybersecurity often require access to vast quantities of data, including sensitive personal information, they raise critical privacy concerns. The ethical quandary here lies in balancing the need for effective security measures against the individual's

right to privacy. AI-driven monitoring tools, while efficient in threat detection, can inadvertently lead to a surveillance state where personal data is constantly analyzed, potentially leading to misuse or unauthorized access.

3. **Transparency and Accountability Issues:** AI's 'black box' nature, where the decision-making process is often opaque, presents significant ethical challenges, especially in a field as critical as cybersecurity. When an AI system makes a decision, such as identifying a network behavior as a threat, the reasoning behind this decision is not always clear. This lack of transparency can lead to distrust and confusion, making it difficult to hold any entity accountable in the event of a failure or a security breach. The question of who bears the responsibility – the AI developers, the cybersecurity team, or the AI system itself – becomes a complex ethical issue.
4. **Autonomy versus Human Oversight:** The increasing autonomy of AI systems in cybersecurity raises questions about the degree of human oversight required. While autonomous systems can efficiently handle vast amounts of data and identify threats faster than human teams, they also reduce the level of human control. This shift can lead to ethical dilemmas, particularly in scenarios where the AI system might make a decision that goes against human judgment or societal norms.
5. **Ethical Use and Misuse of AI:** The potential misuse of AI in cybersecurity by malicious actors is a significant ethical issue. AI systems can be used to develop sophisticated cyber-attacks, creating a scenario where the same technology meant to protect digital assets is used to exploit them. This dual-use nature of AI in cybersecurity necessitates ethical guidelines on the development, distribution, and use of AI technologies to prevent their misuse.

6. **Societal Impact and Trust**: The broader societal impact of AI in cybersecurity cannot be overlooked. Public trust in digital systems and technology at large can be significantly affected by how AI is used in cybersecurity. Ethical use of AI that respects privacy ensures fairness, and is transparent in its operations is crucial in maintaining public trust. Conversely, misuse or opaque functioning of AI systems can lead to a general distrust in technology, affecting not just cybersecurity but the acceptance of AI in other domains.

8.2. Compliance Issues and Regulatory Considerations in AI and Cybersecurity

The integration of Artificial Intelligence (AI) in cybersecurity introduces significant compliance issues and regulatory considerations that organizations must navigate. As AI technologies evolve and become more ingrained in cybersecurity practices, they intersect with a complex and often evolving legal landscape. This intersection raises several key considerations:

1. **Adherence to Data Protection Laws:** The use of AI in cybersecurity often involves the processing of large volumes of data, including sensitive personal information. Ensuring compliance with data protection laws such as the General Data Protection Regulation (GDPR) in Europe, the California Consumer Privacy Act (CCPA) in the United States, and other regional data protection laws is crucial. These laws regulate how personal data can be collected, processed, and stored, imposing strict rules on consent, data subject rights, and data breach notifications. Non-compliance can result in substantial fines and reputational damage, making it essential for cybersecurity AI systems to be designed and operated within these legal frameworks.
2. **Global Compliance Challenges:** Cybersecurity is a global

concern, and AI-driven solutions often need to operate across multiple jurisdictions. This poses a significant challenge as different countries have varying regulations regarding data protection, cyber operations, and AI usage. Organizations must ensure that their AI systems comply not only with the regulations of the country in which they are based but also with those of any other countries where they operate or process data.

3. **Sector-Specific Regulations:** Certain industries are subject to specific regulatory requirements that impact the use of AI in cybersecurity. For instance, the financial sector is governed by regulations like the Sarbanes-Oxley Act (SOX) and the Gramm-Leach-Bliley Act (GLBA), which impose requirements on data protection and reporting of cyber incidents. Healthcare organizations must comply with the Health Insurance Portability and Accountability Act (HIPAA), which includes stringent rules on the handling of health information. These sector-specific regulations can dictate not only how AI systems handle data but also how they report and respond to cybersecurity incidents.
4. **Emerging AI Regulations:** As AI technology advances, governments and international bodies are increasingly focusing on creating AI-specific regulations. These emerging regulations aim to address concerns around fairness, accountability, transparency, and ethical use of AI. Organizations employing AI in cybersecurity must stay informed about these emerging regulations and be prepared to adapt their practices accordingly. This is particularly challenging given the pace at which AI technology evolves compared to the typically slower pace of legislative developments.
5. **Ethical Frameworks and Self-Regulation:** In addition to

legal compliance, there is a growing emphasis on ethical frameworks and self-regulation in the use of AI in cybersecurity. Guidelines and standards proposed by professional bodies like IEEE or ACM, or industry-specific guidelines, offer frameworks for responsible AI deployment. These cover aspects such as ethical design, bias mitigation, transparency, and accountability. While not legally binding, these frameworks often influence public perception and can guide regulatory developments. Adhering to these guidelines can help organizations anticipate regulatory shifts and build public trust.

6. **Contractual and Third-Party Compliance:** The use of third-party AI solutions in cybersecurity introduces additional compliance considerations. Organizations must ensure that their contracts with AI service providers and vendors align with regulatory requirements and industry standards. This includes provisions for data handling, incident reporting, and liability in the event of a breach or failure.
7. **Risk Management and Insurance**: With the growing reliance on AI in cybersecurity, risk management strategies need to be updated to reflect the unique risks associated with AI technologies. This includes assessing the potential for AI failures or breaches and understanding the insurance implications. Cybersecurity insurance policies may need to be reviewed and updated to cover AI-specific risks.

CONCLUSION

The journey through "AUTONOMOUS SECURITY: THE RISE OF AI IN SELF-DEFENDING NETWORKS" has provided a comprehensive exploration of how artificial intelligence (AI) is revolutionizing the field of cybersecurity. As we conclude, it's essential to recapitulate the key takeaways from this exploration and consider the future outlook of AI in cybersecurity.

Key Takeaways:

1. **AI's Transformative Role in Cybersecurity:** AI has dramatically changed how we approach cybersecurity. By automating threat detection and response, AI has enhanced the efficiency, accuracy, and speed of cybersecurity operations, allowing for real-time threat analysis and proactive defense mechanisms.
2. **Evolution of Network Security:** The evolution from traditional, manual cybersecurity practices to AI-driven autonomous security marks a significant shift. This transition highlights the need for continuous learning and adaptation in the face of evolving cyber threats.
3. **Challenges and Ethical Considerations:** While AI presents vast opportunities in cybersecurity, it also brings challenges such as bias in AI algorithms, privacy concerns, transparency, and accountability issues. Ethical considerations are paramount, ensuring that AI systems are fair and unbiased and respect user privacy.
4. **Compliance and Regulatory Landscape:** Navigating the complex web of compliance and regulatory issues is crucial. As AI technology advances, staying abreast of and compliant with international data protection laws, industry-specific regulations, and emerging AI legislation is essential.

Future Outlook:

1. **Continued AI Advancements:** The field of AI is rapidly evolving, promising more advanced and sophisticated AI tools for cybersecurity. Future developments may include enhanced machine learning algorithms capable of predicting and neutralizing threats even more efficiently.
2. **Increased Integration of AI**: As AI technologies become more accessible and affordable, their integration into cybersecurity strategies will likely become more widespread, even among smaller organizations.
3. **Focus on Ethical AI Development:** There will be a growing emphasis on developing AI in an ethical manner. This includes creating AI systems that are transparent, accountable, and free from biases, aligning with both ethical norms and regulatory requirements.
4. **Adaptive Regulatory Frameworks**: The legal landscape surrounding AI in cybersecurity is expected to evolve, with more comprehensive regulations addressing the unique challenges posed by AI technologies. Organizations will need to be flexible and adaptive to stay compliant.
5. **Collaboration and Global Efforts:** Addressing cybersecurity challenges in the age of AI will require global collaboration. Sharing knowledge, best practices, and threat intelligence across borders and industries will be key to effectively

combating cyber threats.

Final Thoughts:

As we look to the future, the role of AI in cybersecurity is not just promising but essential. The journey towards fully autonomous security networks is ongoing and will require continuous innovation, ethical consideration, and regulatory adaptation. By embracing AI's potential while conscientiously addressing its challenges, we can forge a path towards a more secure and resilient digital world.

This book has aimed to provide a foundation for understanding this dynamic field, offering insights into current practices and a vision for the future. The hope is that it serves as both a resource and an inspiration for those at the forefront of navigating and shaping the future of AI in cybersecurity.

GLOSSARY

1. Adversarial AI: Techniques used to manipulate AI systems into making errors by feeding them deceptive inputs.
2. Algorithmic Bias: Prejudice or unfairness in AI decision-making, often due to biased training data or flawed algorithm design.
3. Anomaly Detection: The process of identifying unusual patterns or behaviors in data, signaling potential security incidents or system anomalies.
4. Artificial Intelligence (AI): A field of computer science dedicated to creating intelligent machines capable of performing tasks that require human intelligence.
5. Automated Threat Intelligence and Response Systems: Cybersecurity systems that use automation and advanced analytics for proactive threat identification and response.
6. Autonomous Security: Security systems that operate independently using AI and ML, detecting, analyzing, and responding to threats without human intervention.
7. Biometrics: The measurement and statistical analysis of people's unique physical and behavioral characteristics, often used for identification and access control.
8. Blockchain: A distributed ledger technology known for its robustness and decentralization, often used for securing transactions and data integrity.

9. Blockchain for Network Security: The application of blockchain technology to enhance data integrity and security in network systems.
10. Cloud Computing: Delivery of computing services over the internet to offer faster innovation, flexible resources, and economies of scale.
11. Cloud-based Security Solutions: Security services and infrastructures hosted on cloud platforms, offering scalability, flexibility, and access to advanced security tools.
12. Cryptography: The art of secure communication using codes and ciphers to protect information from unauthorized access.
13. Cybersecurity: The practice of protecting systems, networks, and data from digital attacks.
14. Cybersecurity Frameworks: Structured sets of guidelines and best practices for managing and mitigating cyber risks and threats.
15. Data Breach: An incident where confidential, sensitive, or protected information is accessed or disclosed in an unauthorized manner.
16. Data Encryption: The process of converting sensitive data into a coded format to prevent unauthorized access.
17. Deep Learning: An advanced subset of machine learning involving neural networks, capable of processing and learning from large datasets.
18. Digital Forensics: The practice of recovering and investigating material found in digital devices, often used in the context of cybersecurity.
19. Edge Computing: A distributed computing paradigm that brings computation and data storage closer to data sources, enhancing security and reducing latency.
20. Endpoint Security: Security measures focused on protecting end-user devices like computers, mobile devices, and IoT

devices from cyber threats.

21. Ethical and Privacy Concerns in AI: Issues related to the ethical use of AI in decision-making and the protection of personal data.
22. Ethical Hacking: Authorized attempt to breach the security of a system to identify potential vulnerabilities.
23. Firewall: A network security device that monitors and controls incoming and outgoing network traffic based on security rules.
24. Gradient-based Attacks: Cyber attacks that manipulate the gradient of an AI model's loss function to cause misclassifications or errors.
25. Heuristic Analysis: A technique used in antivirus software to detect new or unknown viruses by examining code behavior and characteristics.
26. Incident Response Plans: Strategies and procedures for identifying, managing, and mitigating cybersecurity incidents.
27. Intrusion Detection System (IDS): Software or devices that monitor networks or systems for malicious activity or policy violations.
28. IoT Security: Measures and technologies used to protect Internet of Things devices and networks from cyber threats.
29. Machine Learning (ML): A subset of AI involving algorithms that learn from data and make predictions or decisions based on that data.
30. Machine Learning Security: Security measures and considerations specifically focused on protecting machine learning systems from cyber threats.
31. Malware: Malicious software designed to damage, disrupt, or gain unauthorized access to computer systems.
32. Neural Networks: AI models inspired by the human brain,

used in machine learning to process complex data.

33. Network Security: Practices and policies designed to prevent and monitor unauthorized access, misuse, modification, or denial of a computer network and its resources.
34. Pattern Recognition: AI's ability to identify patterns and anomalies in data to detect potential cybersecurity breaches.
35. Phishing: A cybercrime involving deceptive communications, typically emails, aimed at stealing sensitive data like passwords and credit card numbers.
36. Predictive Analytics: Using AI to analyze past data and trends to predict future events or threats.
37. Predictive Cybersecurity: AI-driven approaches for anticipating and mitigating future cyber threats.
38. Quantum Computing: A form of computing using quantum-mechanical phenomena, such as superposition and entanglement, for data processing.
39. Quantum Cryptography: Advanced cryptographic techniques leveraging quantum mechanics, used to secure data against quantum computing threats.
40. Real-Time Threat Intelligence: Continuous monitoring and analysis of network data to identify and respond to threats as they occur.
41. Reinforcement Learning: A type of machine learning where an agent learns to behave in an environment by performing actions and seeing the results.
42. Risk Assessment: The process of identifying, analyzing, and evaluating risks, particularly in the context of cybersecurity threats and vulnerabilities.
43. Self-Defending Networks: Networks designed to autonomously detect, prevent, and mitigate cyber threats.
44. Smart Contracts in Cybersecurity: Blockchain-based contracts for automating security responses and policy

enforcement.

45. Social Engineering: Manipulative tactics used to deceive individuals into divulging confidential or personal information for fraudulent purposes.
46. Supervised Learning in AI: A machine learning technique where models are trained on labeled data to recognize and respond to known threats.
47. Transferability: In cybersecurity, the concept that an adversarial attack developed for one AI system can be effective against another similar system.
48. Unsupervised Learning in AI: AI models that learn to identify patterns and anomalies without relying on pre-labeled data, crucial for detecting new or evolving cyber threats.
49. User and Entity Behavior Analytics (UEBA): The use of analytics to understand typical user and entity behaviors in a network to identify anomalies indicative of security threats.
50. Virtual Private Network (VPN): A technology that creates a secure and encrypted connection over a less secure network like the internet.
51. Zero-Day Exploit: A cyber-attack targeting a software vulnerability that is unknown to those who would be interested in mitigating the vulnerability.

About the Author

Valarian Couch is an esteemed cybersecurity expert, mastering the art of safeguarding against evolving cyber threats. With over 15 years of experience, Valarian has a proven track record in enhancing IT infrastructure security and performance. He is known for his innovative solutions, contributing significantly to improvements in cost savings and user retention.

A passionate advocate for digital privacy and online safety, Valarian's expertise extends beyond professional realms, enriching the global community through insightful writings and unwavering support for open-source initiatives. A respected leader, Valarian excels in fostering team collaboration and exceeding organizational goals.

www.ingramcontent.com/pod-product-compliance
Lightning Source LLC
LaVergne TN
LVHW100146061126
851857LV00010B/257
* 9 7 9 8 2 2 3 9 7 2 8 8 4 *